True Faith and Allegiance

True Faith and Allegiance

An American Paratrooper and the 1972 Battle for An Loc

MIKE MCDERMOTT

THE UNIVERSITY OF ALABAMA PRESS
Tuscaloosa

The University of Alabama Press
Tuscaloosa, Alabama 35487-0380
uapress.ua.edu

Hardcover edition published 2012.
Paperback edition published 2024.
eBook edition published 2012.

Inquiries about reproducing material from this work should be addressed to the
University of Alabama Press.

Typeface: Minion & Goudy Sans

Cover image: South Vietnamese soldiers celebrate the destruction of an enemy
T-54 tank that they destroyed inside the friendly perimeter during the 1972 battle
for the provincial capital of An Loc; courtesy of Pham, vnafmamn
Cover design: Todd Lape / Lape Designs

Paperback ISBN: 978-0-8173-6133-4

A previous edition of this book has been cataloged by the Library of Congress.
ISBN: 978-0-8173-1755-3 (cloth)
E-ISBN: 978-0-8173-8583-5

This book is a tribute to all those Vietnamese paratroopers and American airborne advisors who engaged the enemy with courage, dedication, and élan. Asking for little, they were prepared to sacrifice all when dangerous duty called. God bless them and keep them, each and every one.

1. Two South Vietnamese paratroopers in combat. Note the pressure bandage attached to the soldier's helmet. Photo courtesy of Pham, vnafmamn.

Contents

Illustrations

Preface and Acknowledgments

This story chronicles a two-part journey that has been more of an arduous, multi-decade slog than I initially intended. The first phase of the trip took place in Vietnam a long time ago when I committed to an American promise, a national pledge that eventually turned sour. That first lap was also a great personal adventure, a risky undertaking that ended in a sense of loss that continues to dog my steps. The second and much-longer leg of the journey has been years in the making, and it continues to develop. With the insight time allows I've come to realize how much my personal world rests on the foundations laid during those earlier, more-intense days. This book is an examination of some of the connective tissues binding my conflicted present to the formative past—it recognizes consequences.

Only soldiers who fought in those last but little-reported cataclysmic battles of America's war in Vietnam can tell this kind of story. The year 1972 was a confusing and stressful time when the United States was turning away from Indochina and abandoning millions of people who had put their trust in our promises. Despite this country's change of direction, a few American spear-carriers refused to walk away from long-standing commitments. We were the warriors who chose to continue the fight that was not over, even though it was being abandoned by America's leaders.[1]

In those final days before the roof finally fell in on the non-communist peoples of Indochina, I and a few others of a like persuasion remained focused on giving the commissars from North Vietnam a bloody nose. We were the last American soldiers to fight in that war, and it was a historic moment when we and our South Vietnamese warrior brothers joined hands to defeat the invading enemy on an extremely lethal battlefield.

As I began the process of recalling those long-ago events, I first focused on a few vivid recollections that proved to be the tips of mental icebergs floating mostly beneath the surface. It took time and effort to tease long-suppressed memories and emotions into revealing themselves more clearly. Much like the proverbial onion that brings tears before eventually contributing to a savory outcome, writing this book has required peeling back the layers. At times discomforting, the process has also been restorative and rewarding.

Restorative in the sense I began to better remember a noble cause I once volunteered to serve. I'd forgotten how strongly I felt about joining the fight in Vietnam, how sure I was that it was the right thing to do. As the writing process unfolded I began to rediscover that idealistic young soldier, the one full of joyful energy and a thirst for adventure who answered an invitation to participate in a great crusade. The intervening years have taught many lessons, but prominent among them—I once had the courage to embrace a noble and worthy mission, a morally significant undertaking, a thrilling leap I would never be able to repeat.

While many of those rediscoveries have been rewarding, pulling up long-submerged memories has not been therapeutic in every instance. I've been reminded that the hard-boiled soldier of yesteryear is still there, lurking just out of sight, regardless of persistent efforts to sweeten him up under layers of social lipstick to get him house-broken. For the first time in years I got a good look at the rascal, peering out from the shadows as I worked to resurrect some of the most intimate and painful kinds of events a soldier can experience.

Those recollections sometimes caught me with an unexpected jolt. For a moment I would be that old self again, back in those desperate times when men were slipping through a portal just beyond my reach, a window that had suddenly opened, but only for those who were called. Somehow I had forgotten the feeling of terrible finality, the pain of wishing Godspeed to men who were leaving while I remained behind. How could I have forgotten those times when eternity beckoned through machine-gun fire? How did I become so careless that I let my most significant life experience lose its edge?

I didn't always expect to survive, but here I am, living with it. I must tell you, however, that I'm not trudging along as I once did, flying solo inside my own head. I'm connecting with others in healthful ways and much of that positive change has developed through the process of recovering that important part of my life, that first arduous lap.

To all who have honored me with their friendship and encouragement, please accept my sincere and heartfelt gratitude. I treasure the lift and fun you bring to living. It's also important for me to recognize Carl Brandt, Dan Ross, and Dan Waterman; their insightful and tempered guidance has been instrumental in bringing this project to fruition. Without their encouragement this book would have remained a frustrated manuscript hidden away on a closet shelf. But of paramount importance, first and last and with all my heart, I ask blessings for my loving and understanding Chulan. She is the one who gives me hope and purpose; she keeps me between the ditches.

True Faith and Allegiance

I

An Introduction to the Past

Raised in a small town in rural South Dakota, the eldest of five kids who grew up in a secure and supportive family nest, I was ready to spread my wings when the time came. My mother and father were very decent and honorable people, devout and sincere. They loved each other and lived out their dream of how they thought being married and creating a family should be. They valued education and recognized achievement. They set limits and enforced the rules. They also understood slackers and gave whiney behavior short shrift.

Good friends to their neighbors, my folks had a sense of humor and enjoyed life despite the daily stresses and strains of keeping it all on track. Most of the big issues, the world-class perplexities, were presented as reassuringly straightforward and clear-cut. The answers tended toward black or white with little need for ambiguity. One of the many truths my brothers and sisters and I absorbed held that America's virtues were an inspiration to humankind everywhere. We knew deep in our bones that being an American was something special. We Americans held ourselves to a higher standard. Although our leaders might occasionally reveal a human foible, they were committed to correct directions, wonderfully selfless and true. The ideals I absorbed at my parents' dinner table reflected the confidence of a triumphant post-WWII America and my patriotism developed early. It took years for cracks to appear in the worldview of my youth.

I first arrived in South Vietnam in June 1967 and joined the 1st Brigade of the famous 101st Airborne Division. My appearance was something of a homecoming; I'd previously served in the division at Ft. Campbell as an enlisted paratrooper before finishing college. Returning to the 101st reunited me with old comrades who insisted on seeking me out. They thought it hilarious to salute a former sergeant who had reappeared wearing a new lieutenant's shiny gold bars. An infantry platoon leader's job and later a rifle company commander's responsibilities were something I understood and loved doing. Serving as a company grade infantry officer in combat was a terrific adventure, providing the most soul-testing challenges and deeply fulfilling satisfactions imaginable.

When the events described in this book took place I'd just completed three years in Vietnam with the 101st Airborne Division. Those tours entailed a lot of slogging through rice paddies and living in mountainous jungles for months at a time. I'd participated in a number of major battles to include Tet 1968 when my unit initially fought in the outskirts of Saigon before joining the battle to recapture Hue. That bloody affair was followed by a bruising campaign to clear the major road west from Hue to the A Shau Valley on the Laotian border. I was involved in other campaigns out on the Cambodian border as well as in the far northern parts of the country. In 1971 I was at Khe Sanh when the firebase and runway were reactivated for the South Vietnamese army's disastrous incursion into Laos.

During those years the harsh realities of combat were repeatedly reinforced by deadly encounters with the enemy that were always sobering and occasionally horrendous. Over time my sense of personal adventure matured and developed into a professionalism rooted in my service to the army and the nation.

I felt that my commitment, as well as the sacrifices made by many of my comrades, was validated by Washington's support for Indochina in general and South Vietnam in particular. The size and duration of this country's effort reinforced the political rhetoric; the assistance the United States provided over a series of administrations influenced my decision to commit to the long haul. As a result I found myself living out one of my mother's favorite dictums, which held that actions speak louder than words. But by late 1971, with my third tour completed, it had become crystal clear the Nixon administration was pulling the plug on Indochina. In fact America's departure had become a stampede for the exit, leaving mountains and oceans of materials for our erstwhile allies to absorb whether they were ready or able or not.

Even though the American army, to include the 101st Airborne Division, was pulling out, my fidelity to the mission remained as it had been. The purpose of the fight I'd embraced years before had not changed. A disinterested observer might have labeled me a romantic with an itch to stay in lock step with the last centurions, or just stubborn and brassbound, and perhaps there's a bit of truth to be found there. But in fact I gave my options a lot of serious thought, and after much soul searching decided that remaining involved was the right thing for me. So rather than quitting Vietnam and returning home with my unit, I volunteered to stay as an advisor with the Vietnamese Airborne Division.

Vietnamese paratroopers were justifiably recognized as elite professionals who had consistently fought the toughest battles since their creation during the earlier French Indochina War. American soldiers serving with the Vietnamese Airborne Division were members of Advisory Team 162, a small organization of dedicated professionals who fought alongside their tough and valiant Vietnamese comrades. I admired everything I knew about the Vietnamese Airborne as well as the American advisors serving with them, and I was honored to be counted among their number.

Meanwhile, the North Vietnamese enemy had been stalling the peace talks in Paris while they watched America slipping out the back door in Indochina, and they recognized a new and welcome opportunity when they saw one. In fact they were being presented with an opening hard to ignore. Having long predicted the United States didn't have the stomach to persevere, the enemy prepared a massive military invasion to be delivered on three fronts. They crafted a series of surprises intended to embarrass the weakened foreigners while possibly overwhelming the Saigon government, and their offensive arrived as a rude shock for both the Americans and the South Vietnamese.

But those battles were still to come. In January 1972 South Vietnam was enjoying a period of relative tranquility. The countryside was more secure and peaceful than it had been for years even though everyone there understood the war was not over. Unknown to me, North Vietnam was even then busily shifting large conventional forces to include artillery and armor units into their base areas along the Demilitarized Zone separating North and South. They were working equally hard to move the same kinds of forces down the Ho Chi Minh Trail and into their sanctuaries in Laos and Cambodia, areas immediately adjacent to South Vietnam's western borders.

The lull in the war came to a sudden and dramatic end when the North Vietnamese launched their attacks during the last week of March 1972. They opened a spectacular new chapter in the war that proved to be a serious upshift from previous levels of ground combat. Because of the timing, their campaign soon became known as the Easter Offensive and quickly developed into a series of full-blown and bloody slugging matches. The enemy managed to seize and hold some territory, but their larger strategic goal of ending the war by seizing Saigon[1] was frustrated by a South Vietnamese army that defended the strategic approaches to the capital with tenacity. A critically important element in the defender's equation was a cadre of American advisors backed up by a massive volume of American air power; that extraordinarily effective team made all the difference for South Vietnam.

As the full scope of the Easter Offensive began to unfold, the soldiers of the Vietnamese Airborne Division and their American advisors were ordered into the very eye of the typhoon. The Vietnamese paratroopers I served with seemed to initially view the developing battles as just another chapter in a long and drawn-out war with no foreseeable end. For many of the American advisors, particularly those veterans who had served multiple combat tours, the opening rounds of the offensive looked a bit like what Yogi Berra once described as deja vu all over again. Very quickly, however, the size, intensity, and lethality of those new battlefields promised combat on a dramatically elevated level. As the war was beginning to fade from televisions in the United States, the last American soldiers to fight in Vietnam were engulfed in a series of high-intensity battles exceeding anything previously experienced in that war.

My story of service with the Vietnamese Airborne is presented as a series of reminiscences, memories of happenings long ago that I offer on behalf of all who wore the tiger-striped uniform and the maroon beret. We who served with Advisory Team 162 will never forget our Vietnamese paratrooper brothers. They demonstrated a special kind of dedication and courage throughout the long years of a war that, for them, started in 1946 and ended in 1975. They were consistently tough and resilient no matter the odds they faced, the support they received, or their battlefield prospects.

I have included the names of several participants in these vignettes, men I became acquainted with during the battle for An Loc. Military ranks mentioned are as of the spring of 1972. While it was tempting to create conversations to dramatize and personalize some of the events described, I resisted the urge to put words in anyone's mouth. In fact I'm not at all sure what I might have said forty years ago either.

As I think back to those days of commitment and action it's hard to believe so much time has passed since I last saw Vietnam, the place where I pledged myself to a righteous cause and where I and so many others were betrayed by the American government. Over the years I've learned the ghosts may slumber, but they cannot die.

2
The Current State of Play

I can hear rain on the skylight. Not hard, but persistent, but that's not what woke me. I always come awake in our bedroom totally alert, every night, no fuzziness, no confusion. I know exactly where I am and what's around me even though it's dark. My wife, my delicately beautiful Chulan, is within easy reach under the covers. I can hear and feel her breathing. What a marvelous security I have found with her. A wondrous comfort, but it's 3:00 A.M. and it's time for me to move.

I need to patrol the perimeter. There was a time, not so long ago, when I would slip through the alley door and be out in the yard. I would find myself on the quiet nighttime sidewalks, standing beside a tree, scanning. But things have changed over the past couple of years, my patrols have narrowed. My Chulan has made me a gift of great value. She has introduced me to a new sense of wellness, slowly growing, becoming more solid, more complete. The rain has begun to pound and the yard is swimming, the patio and streets are alive with bouncing water. One of my current posts is at the side of the dining room window, another at the edge of the back door. Loaded with hollow points, my snub-nose pistol pulls at the pocket of my bathrobe, never needed but always ready. I'm standing right next to the rain, a foot from the downpour, dry and warm, not lying soaked and chilled in the jungle. I watch the shadows in the back yard, and although I wait, nothing moves.

Back up the stairs with the bedroom door relocked behind me. Finding the warmth of my wife in the center of our special private place, pulling the feather comforter over us both, stretching full length and grinning with the miracle of my deliverance, my good fortune. Chulan's small warm feet move and find me. She's deep in sleep, my loving and trusting woman, but still offering the reassurance we both seek.

We first met in the ancient city of Zibo, a historic center for ceramics on the Yellow River floodplain south of Beijing. Chulan had been a progeny in her father's work unit, the first girl selected to attend an engineering university since Liberation in 1949. I was floundering in the aftermath of a disastrously painful divorce, but had traveled to China as something of an act of faith and taken the train down from Beijing. It was during the Chinese New Year's Festival and the train was crowded. Chulan greeted me at the station and took me to her parish church. She wanted me to meet her community of Catholic friends, good people who were expecting us.

The taxi stopped on a side street under construction and we threaded our way between piles of dirt and sewer pipe to a narrow gate in a concrete wall. Once inside the churchyard we saw the priest holding court with a small circle of parishioners, sitting out of the wind on plastic chairs. Someone in the group pointed us out as we stepped through the gate and Father Goh came trotting, arms spread wide in greeting. Middle aged and chubby in a tattered cassock and worn-out shoes, he was a survivor of work camps, the abuses of the Cultural Revolution, and the years of repression before the churches were allowed to reopen. He embraced and blessed Chulan and welcomed me into his world of faith. We'd brought a fancy wicker basket of oranges that was quickly passed to a Sister for distribution. Holding my hands, Father Goh wanted to know if I'd ever visited Chicago. He asked that the next time I was there to please tell the priests, who had first established his parish, to remember and return. He needs them, and he prays for them daily.

And finally, after repeated trips to China, Chulan agreed to join me in America. We were married in the presence of my children with a Jesuit friend officiating, and much has happened since that memorable day. Although Chulan had studied English for years in China, she had only spoken with other Chinese and wanted to improve her language skills at a local community college. Those first academic efforts in a new society, struggling with an ever more complex level of vocabulary and usage, quickly expanded into mastering the prerequisites for a more ambitious goal. Her math and science professors were impressed by her abilities and encouraged her to consider an advanced degree. Chulan applied for admittance to two Doctor of Pharmacy programs. She was interviewed by both, and accepted by both, and that triumph introduced me to another level of my new wife's abilities. It also pointed the next step in our journey together.

Chulan is my perfect counter. She has brought a balanced insight, a steadiness of purpose, a reminder of life's riches, a renewal of spiritual joy, a reaffirmation of the timeless values I had abandoned. She has fostered and nurtured a process of healing in my life, something I despaired of ever accomplishing on my own. Chulan has convinced me that I am trusted. She loves and accepts me. She allows me to love and protect her in return. I can be a responsible husband without the drama of false competitions and silly accusations I'd come to associate with marriage. She finds pleasure and humor in daily events and relationships, and she looks to the future with great faith. I recognized her and wanted her in my life on the very first day we met, and now I am able to sleep after securing the perimeter.

I know my life should be easier at this point, my spirit less troubled and my emotions less conflicted. I should have found some of the serenity that age and experience is supposed to grant, but that's not the way it is. I'm on edge, waiting for the unexpected, the sudden problem I must be prepared to immediately jump on and fix. I'm ready for the intruder, the oncoming car wandering across the centerline, the hidden hole, ceaselessly alert to all the dangers my mind is forever creating. My overworked mind, constantly one jump ahead of the mundane reality that never produces the emergencies I'm primed to confront. But when the door slams or the phone jars me, I'm tensed for the fight, heart hammering, measuring and ready to nail the threat.

Underlying and nurturing these symptoms is a deeper and in many ways a much more serious issue, one that has eaten away at me for years. When I was young I committed to a life-changing experience by acting on an invitation to pay any price, bear any burden, meet any hardship, support any friend, oppose any foe, in order to assure the survival and success of liberty. I accepted that call to action broadcast by a president to a receptive nation. By taking that fateful step I, along with tens of thousands of my generation, embraced an obligation of service, a career of duty that for me found its initial focus in America's war in Vietnam.

Over time I've learned that by the very nature of things, commitments change. The ability to keep our balance when life's tectonic plates shift is an acquired skill, and critical for survival, but it's important to recognize that there is always a price to pay for every decision made—better that our choices rest firmly on ethical principals. With the passing years I've gained a deeper appreciation of my mother's persistent caution: don't do something you wouldn't want to discuss at home. I'm not proud of everything I did in combat—despite all my enthusiasms, the damage and killing I managed to accomplish did not change the eventual outcome of the war by a single scintilla. The best I can say for myself is that I survived and learned. I'm also not proud of how the United States conducted itself vis-à-vis the responsibilities it assumed in Indochina. This country betrayed itself when it betrayed that trust, and the self-inflicted wounds are deep and long lasting. Aeschylus, a man who wrote from considerable personal experience, captured the flavor of these conflicted transactions more than 2,500 years ago:

He who learns must suffer.
And even in our sleep
pain that cannot forget
falls drop by drop upon the heart,
and in our own despair,
against our will,
comes wisdom
by the awful grace of God.[1]

3
Welcome to Team 162 and the Vietnamese Airborne

The Vietnamese Airborne Division's headquarters was located inside the high perimeter fence on the military side of Tan Son Nhut Airport, a sprawling facility enmeshed in Saigon's much more extensive sprawl. The city never even pretended to sleep. Its teeming and filthy streets were jammed with every type of vehicle competing with crowds of people meandering, running, squatting, gawking, spitting, screaming at each other, eating from the roadside food stalls, buying and selling everything under the sun, and living out their lives largely in public view. But the out-of-control confusion ended at the gates of Tan Son Nhut, except for the civilian terminal buildings where airline tickets were at a premium and competition was fierce. Reputed to be the busiest airport in the world, Tan Son Nhut was alive with an unending stream of airliners, fighter planes, cargo planes, helicopters, and every variety of private aircraft congesting and crisscrossing the airways. The airport was so large that the Vietnamese Airborne Division headquarters, located a mile or more from the unremitting thunder of the active runways, seemed half asleep.

I arrived at the front gates of Tan Son Nhut during the last week of January 1972 and was met by a Vietnamese paratrooper driving an Airborne Division jeep. After saluting and throwing my duffle bag in the back we roared off down a street that led away from the main part of the airport. The ride took us through areas littered with assorted trash and leaking oil drums, abandoned hangars, and various dilapidated buildings. We bounced across stretches of fractured tarmac and crumbling concrete overgrown with weeds, baking in the sun. Along our route I saw several airplane junkyards overflowing with vandalized wrecks that traced the whole history of aviation in Southeast Asia. Several times during the drive I noticed bunkers encrusted with sandbags partially melted by the monsoon rains. Weed-choked barbed-wire fences also wandered off into the clutter toward the backside of the base. On some of those fences I glimpsed an occasional rusty metal sign with a skull and crossbones and the word MINE stenciled in red. I'd had several very sobering experiences with land mines in the past and those signs gave me the willies. Just the idea that some of those deadly things had been planted and lost in the depths of the trashy airfield made me sweat.

A corporal's guard of Vietnamese paratroopers was posted at the main gate of the fenced-off Airborne Division headquarters. Their salutes were sharp as they waved my jeep through their checkpoint. The buildings inside the compound were French colonial in style, solid one- and two-story concrete structures with red-tile roofs. They were painted in fading ochre and scattered across an area the size of several city blocks. The buildings all sported heavy wooden shutters latched open to encourage circulation as there didn't seem to be any air conditioning. The whole area appeared to be slumbering in the heat under the spreading limbs of enormous banyan trees, each with the bottom four feet of trunk coated in whitewash. Tropical bushes heavy with crimson blossoms grew inside their individual circles of white-painted rocks and more white rocks traced walkways throughout the area. Brightly painted signs were on prominent display and the hard-packed ground had been carefully swept clean with not a scrap or twig to be seen. I couldn't see any people walking around the area either.

Several years before, when I was a lieutenant completing my first tour in Vietnam, I'd visited that same Vietnamese Airborne Division compound. I'd heard good things about the unit and wanted to join the team of American advisors serving with Vietnamese paratroopers. After finding my way to the adjutant's office and explaining my business, I was ushered into the august presence of the division's senior advisor, an American colonel of infantry. The colonel was sitting behind a large and impressive desk wearing tiger-striped fatigues starched stiff and covered with qualification patches. I saluted and reported, and he responded by jumping up and waving me to an old leather sofa where he immediately joined me. The colonel talked for several minutes about the mission of the advisory team, and then produced a 3x5 card that he referenced while outlining the team's personnel authorizations and reviewing the officers assigned in very specific detail.

I was not used to sitting knee-to-knee on creaky old leather sofas with colonels, but I was flattered that he took the time to introduce me to his organization. He stressed that he didn't need another red-hot lieutenant, but he could always use a moxie captain who had commanded a rifle company and could be trusted to make good tactical decisions in the field. He finished up our ten-minute conversation by saying he'd be pleased to have me on his team, but only after I had acquired the necessary experience.

We shook hands and saluted after I thanked him, and then I returned up-country to the 101st Airborne Division to get the seasoning and promotion needed to join Team 162. That colonel had moved on and been replaced several times over, but now I was back, ready to join the soldiers I considered the best of the best.

As soon as the driver parked the jeep in front of the advisor's building I went searching for the adjutant's office. An American personnel clerk was acting busy behind the counter and several Vietnamese secretaries were enjoying a midday siesta at their desks. The adjutant was not available and the division senior advisor was out of the office so the clerk took copies of my orders and signed me into the unit. He also gave me directions to the supply building so I could draw the field gear I would need. The team supply sergeant issued me three sets of tiger-striped fatigues, a rucksack, a nylon poncho liner, the eight canteens I asked for, a helmet, and a rifle. A little Vietnamese lady in a nearby tailor shop sewed the required patches onto my new uniforms and sold me a maroon paratrooper's beret. I loaded my gear into the jeep and the driver delivered me to my new living quarters in Saigon, the Missouri Bachelor Officers Quarters (BOQ).

The personnel clerk had told me most of the team officers were billeted at the Missouri BOQ. My new address was a four-story concrete building that looked like a cross between a fortress and a cheap no-tell hotel. The front gate of the BOQ compound was about fifty yards down a filthy side street distinguished by numerous bicycle shops and two-table cafés selling stale soda, warm beer, and questionable food items displayed under plastic covers. Crowds of people were strolling through puddles of stagnant water and clouds of flies circulated lazily through layered odors in the sticky heat. The compound's wide-open gate was guarded by an elderly and lethargic Vietnamese veteran with a neglected carbine slung over his drooping shoulder. He waved my jeep through with a sloppy salute and an apologetic grin.

The small lobby had a muddy tile floor, a couple of dusty potted plants, and a littered concrete stairwell climbing to the upper levels. After signing in with the clerk at the shabby front desk I carried my gear up to my new lodgings on the third floor. The building had been constructed around an interior courtyard and open walkways sporting ornamental balustrades circled the inside of the building at each level. The BOQ rooms opened off the interior walkways, and my accommodations turned out to be a small concrete box with a cracked and dirty linoleum floor. The tiny bathroom included a commode and a cold water spigot in the corner that shot a jet of nonpotable water out of a corroded pipe at head height. A metal frame bed, a rickety table and chair, and a cheap chest of drawers constituted the furniture. A dingy gray curtain covered the single cloudy and fly-specked window that looked onto the sun-blasted interior courtyard. The overhead fan was operated by a giant metal dial screwed to the wall, located conveniently next to a light switch that operated the single neon tube attached directly over the bed.

I locked my gear in the room and climbed another level to the open air bar and café on the building's flat roof. That rooftop oasis provided a fantastic view across the city. It also offered a welcome breeze under a large parachute canopy stretched to provide shade for the bar. The whole place seemed to float above the dirt and heat of Saigon, and it was a relief to find a comfortable stool and a cold beer. An hour later several other members of Advisory Team 162 appeared. They took turns admiring and complimenting me on my shiny new tiger-striped fatigues and made sure I understood my position as the most recent member of the team. Despite the new-guy jokes it was good to finally meet some of the Americans who were serving with Vietnamese paratroopers. They told me that advisors were in the field with their units most of the time and stressed they spent very little time in Saigon. That certainly turned out to be the case for me as I only stayed a couple of nights at the Missouri BOQ during my tour with the Vietnamese Airborne Division.

My new boss, Major Jack Todd, walked into the rooftop bar about supper time. He was a combat-experienced infantry officer and had just driven up from the National Training Center, which was located several hours by road southeast of Saigon near the seacoast town of Vung Tau. Jack was the senior advisor to the 8th Airborne Battalion, and I soon learned I was to be his assistant. Following a hearty welcome to the team, he took me under his wing. Over a steak and another beer I asked about the division's mission and organization, and Jack confirmed that the Airborne Division was South Vietnam's strategic reserve.

Commanded by a two-star general, the division was under the direct control of the country's national leadership, and its units were committed to combat when hard fighting was required to deal with serious problems. The Airborne Division had earned a well-deserved reputation as the nation's elite, and a number of officers who had cut their teeth in airborne units had gone on to the highest military and political positions in the country. The division was organized much like an American airborne division with three brigade headquarters that provided command and control for the nine infantry battalions as well as artillery, engineer, and other support units.

The three brigades, commanded by colonels, were occasionally reconfigured as their missions changed, but normally a brigade headquarters controlled three infantry battalions plus any additional units necessary to meet mission requirements. The infantry battalions, usually commanded by lieutenant colonels, were organized with a small headquarters company, three rifle companies, and a combat support company with a total strength of approximately five hundred soldiers and thirty officers. In an American battalion the internal companies are designated alphabetically: A Company, B Company, and so forth; but the Vietnamese identified their companies by using the battalion's number followed by a company number. As an example, the 8th Airborne Battalion's headquarters company was 80 Company and the three rifle companies and the combat support companies were numbered 81, 82, 83, and 84, respectively. Jack assured me that airborne battalions were deployed on combat operations somewhere in the country all the time, but very seldom had the division been committed to fight as a single organization.

One of those occasions had occurred the previous year when the division had been part of a disastrous South Vietnamese invasion of Laos intended to disrupt North Vietnamese supply lines. Labeled Lam Son 719, the operation had been supported by American forces to include the 101st Pathfinders, which I had commanded at the time. During that operation the Pathfinders had continued to work the firebase and airmobile missions the 101st was running farther south while also supporting the reopened base at Khe Sanh where the South Vietnamese were marshaled. I had been busy covering all those activities, which spanned some one hundred miles of countryside, but I was present when the South Vietnamese army to include the airborne division went across the border into Laos. I was also there as those units struggled to survive before escaping back across the border once the North Vietnamese concentrated their forces and chased them back into South Vietnam.[1]

Jack went on to tell me the division's 1st Brigade, which included three infantry battalions, had just returned from a series of hard-fought battles along the Cambodian border. The brigade headquarters and its senior advisor, Lieutenant Colonel Art Taylor, was in Saigon, but the three infantry battalions were at the National Training Center undergoing an intensive period of refitting and retraining. Early the next morning Jack and I departed the BOQ and drove out of Saigon to join our battalion.

The main road from Saigon to Vung Tau had recently been rebuilt. It was a modern two-lane hard-topped highway crowded with vehicles of every possible description. Somehow the free-for-all traffic accommodated everyone. Cars, trucks, farm tractors pulling wagons, people on bicycles and meandering on foot, and wandering livestock all shared the road. Everyone swerved together like a school of fish to avoid plowing through occasional stretches of husked rice spread out to dry on plastic sheets along the edges of the hardtop.

There was no sense of threat or danger as we left Saigon and drove into the countryside. I recall being acutely aware of that carefree feeling, particularly when I recognized several places where battles had been fought during Tet 1968 when I was serving with the 101st. The enemy's political infrastructure and the local communist armed forces had been largely destroyed during those fights, when they had ventured out into the open, and as a result of their demise the war was in remission and the countryside was flourishing. Villages and larger towns were humming with commerce and farmers were up to their collective hips in green rice paddies in every direction.

I was delighted with my new assignment and with life in general and looked forward to meeting the other advisors already at the National Training Center. I was also ready to get acquainted with those Vietnamese paratroopers, and based on their reputation I was sure my service with them would be a professional high point. The hard combat of past years seemed remote as we drove down that highway, and the beautiful countryside only reinforced the impression that I was embarking on a fresh new adventure. I knew it was going to be very different from the kind of soldiering I had previously experienced in Vietnam. With my maroon beret pulled down at a jaunty angle I arrived for work, eager to get started. Considering how the war soon developed, it's undoubtedly best that we are shielded from actually reading our futures with much clarity.

4

Side Trips from the National Training Center

The National Training Center was located in the sand dunes and salt marsh wastes about fifteen miles north of Vung Tau. Training areas spread along the beaches of the South China Sea and ran inland for miles. The headquarters area, at the end of a long gravel road, consisted of rows of decaying and sun-bleached plywood buildings grouped around a parade ground sporting its obligatory flagpole. A rifle company from each battalion was required to man bunkers on a perimeter that encircled the headquarters area. Neglected and ramshackle barracks accommodated the rest of the troops, and the entire place appeared to be slowly rotting into the wastes. The National Training Center was a depressing and dismal place with a single function—training troops for combat.

In addition to the three airborne battalions, several Cambodian battalions were also undergoing a training cycle. They had American advisors with them as well. I soon learned the Vietnamese government occasionally provided facilities for Cambodian troops who would return to their own side of the border once their training had been completed. Hopefully they would then be better prepared to fight the Khmer Rouge and North Vietnamese units that were expanding their reach in Cambodia. The South Vietnamese and Cambodian troops were kept separated as the two nationalities had a long and bloody history of conflict and there was no love lost between them. That sense of antipathy and potential trouble kept all the American advisors focused on their own units. The sensitive nature of a Cambodian training mission established another barrier that precluded getting acquainted with those other Americans, whoever they were.

Soon after we arrived, Jack introduced me to the commander of the 8th Airborne Battalion, Lieutenant Colonel Van Ba Ninh. Colonel Ninh was slight built, trim, and very focused on the business at hand, and he made a thoughtful effort to welcome me to the battalion. After returning my salute, shaking hands, and asking me to join him under a sun shade, he inquired about my previous service in Vietnam. Colonel Ninh listened closely and seemed satisfied when I told him I had served three years with the 101st Airborne Division. The fact that I had commanded both a rifle company and the division Pathfinder unit seemed to be a bonus. Although our discussion lasted only a few minutes, I left our meeting convinced that Colonel Ninh was an experienced and tough commander of combat paratroopers.

The three airborne battalions were conducting unit training that would help integrate new soldiers and junior officers into their platoons and companies. The training program emphasized small unit leadership and was focused on reestablishing the cohesion that had eroded because of heavy casualties during recent battles. It seemed that all three battalions needed to rebuild from the ground up. The very fact that all three needed to reconstitute to that extent provided my first clue that Vietnamese paratrooper units accepted high casualty rates as a normal way of doing business. I was to learn a good deal more about their attitude toward combat soon enough. Unit strength continued to build as trucks loaded with new recruits and veterans returning from hospitals pulled in from Saigon every day.

The daily grind at the National Training Center was demanding and rigorous, and the routine was filled with heat, flies, dust, and sweat. Training objectives emphasized small unit operations such as conducting patrols, setting ambushes, and attacking strong points. Training also included calling for and adjusting mortar and artillery fire and establishing defensive positions. Individual and unit security was a major theme stressed in all training.

Sergeants and junior officers were the principal instructors and training was conducted using live ammunition. The Vietnamese Airborne liked to do night operations, and trying to get some sleep during the heat of the day was virtually impossible. Days and nights soon began to blend together. The troops were aggressive and confident, and the chain of command accepted an occasional injury from friendly fire. One evening a rifle company conducting a search operation flushed a half dozen local Viet Cong in the sand dunes and killed several. The battalion commander was delighted. No one had expected the local talent to venture within miles of our training areas. To catch an enemy reconnaissance team trying to track us was particularly satisfying to Colonel Ninh, who felt that killing a few of them added spice to what had become an otherwise bland training event.

The American advisors slept on steel cots in a small shack whose only item of comfort was a much-abused refrigerator. To ensure the beer stayed cold, that ancient machine was hard-wired into a generator located just out-

side the flimsy back wall. The only other luxury was fresh water for showers. The food was local fare, primarily rice and vegetables with some fish or
shredded chicken plus an occasional C-ration, so the daily menu left much
to be desired. After several weeks of sweating with the battalion, Jack seemed
satisfied that our training schedule was on track. He suggested the two of us
take a break and let the unit commanders do their work without our hovering presence, so we commandeered a jeep and decamped to enjoy an afternoon recess in the town of Vung Tau.

Located at the far and breezy tip of what had formerly been known as
Cape St. Jacques, Vung Tau was a jewel of a small seaside resort town. Facing directly onto the beach, it was provincial, tree shaded, quiet, and seemingly isolated from the outside world as time slipped by under a tropical sun.
During the colonial period Vung Tau had been a French playground, and it
retained much of the appearance and many of the airs of those former glory
days with several attractive seafood restaurants and assorted watering holes
along the promenade facing the sea.

We made La Rotisserie, a delightful small French café with a shaded patio, our informal headquarters. From our wicker chairs we watched families
strolling on the beach, kids running and splashing in the shallows, and local fishing boats returning with the day's catch. We also enjoyed the world's
best gin and tonics made at tableside with Beefeaters and Schweppes, served
in tall glasses with tiny sliced limes. The king prawns were fresh from the sea
and served in butter with a bit of garlic. The air was clean and had a strong
salt tang, and the Vietnamese girls strolling hand in hand in the cool of the
late afternoon were elegant and beautiful. They provided a wistful topic of
conversation for a pair of slightly buzzed airborne advisors as we drove back
to our sweltering shack at the training center.

On another hot and dusty afternoon Jack suggested we have supper at a
local resort he had heard about. We'd just completed a long session of evalu-
ating the rifle companies as they maneuvered through a live fire exercise in
the shimmering salt wastes, and a chance to escape the tedium of the advisor's shack sounded like a wonderful idea to me. Although the resort's exact
location wasn't clear, we set off in our jeep to track it down.

A weather-beaten sign on the main highway pointed us down a dirt road
that was soon pressed on both sides by a swamp of stagnant water and high
reed beds. After about a mile of bad road the situation was only getting worse,
and we were ready to retrace our tracks when we got a glimpse of a two-story
building rising out of the distant swamp. Finally driving up to the place,
we discovered the property was surrounded by a fifteen-foot concrete wall
topped with shards of broken glass. The big steel gates were closed. The com-

pound was totally isolated in the middle of a drowned and mosquito-infested wasteland. A faded sign attached to the wall was lettered in Vietnamese, Chinese, and French, but it was not clear if Jack's resort was in operation or even occupied.

I got out of the jeep and banged on the gates, eventually getting a response from the other side. First a peephole was slid open and slammed shut, then hinges squealed as the rusty gates were pulled back by a surly and seedy guard. He appeared to be about fifty years old with salt and pepper hair braided in a long pigtail down his back. Clad in a gray T-shirt, shorts, and shower shoes, he sported a pair of snaky eyes, a drooping mustachio, and a well-oiled automatic rifle. In appearance and attitude he was perfectly type cast as a river pirate, which may have been closer to the truth than we would ever know. Jack drove the jeep into an enclosed compound that looked more like a construction site than a resort parking lot, and the guard horsed the gates shut.

Piles of sand, stacks of cement block, and several abused dump trucks were pushed against the inside walls. The resort was a raw, two-story cement building whose construction was a bit short of completion. We were met at the front steps by a chubby Chinese-Vietnamese gentleman, turned out in an incongruous white cotton suit and tie. He assured us the place was open for business, and his delight at our arrival oozed from every pore. He grinned and bobbed. Velly welcome—Velly welcome—Pleesss to come in. The place seemed to be unoccupied except for the guard and the suit and possibly someone in the kitchen, assuming that the two guys didn't also do the cooking.

The whole place was surreal, baking in the heat and humidity. The lack of habitation and the sense of isolation also made it a little spooky. Our host ushered us through an echoing lobby and up a sweep of concrete stairs to the second floor. He then led us into an enormous banquet room of monochrome white tile, filled with large round plastic tables and dozens of chairs. The cavernous room reverberated as we threaded our way to a table at the far end. Our chosen spot was next to an open window where we could keep an eye on our jeep in the courtyard below. Our gear was piled underfoot with our rifles in easy reach as we looked over an elaborate menu.

Multipaged and printed in Vietnamese and Chinese, it soon became clear the menu was totally bogus when our host had to admit our dining options were either fish or steak. Jack and I agreed the steak option was a classic example of the kind of mystery meat best avoided whenever possible. At least we had some idea where the fish might have originated, so that was our unanimous choice. After many tiny cups of hot green tea, the fish, about three feet long and sporting quarter-size silver scales, was delivered reclining on a massive steel platter. It appeared as bemused as we were, goggling at us from its tepid broth. We set about exploring its possibilities with a large aluminum spoon and plastic chopsticks. A chipped porcelain bowl of gritty steamed rice and more tea completed the meal, so polishing off dinner didn't take very long.

We could see over the compound walls from our second-story window and what we saw was not encouraging. Our resort was literally at the end of the road and the swamp stretched on as far as the eye could see through drifting mist and clouds of mosquitoes. The back wall of the compound was on the banks of a broad and muddy river that hadn't been apparent from ground level. Although the sun was nearing the far horizon it was hot and the humidity had to be approaching 100 percent.

We were both uncomfortable with the whole harebrained situation. There was only one way back out of that place, and the impulse to get energized became more compelling with each succeeding cup of tea. I had no idea how our preposterous maitre d'hotel actually made a living, considering the scant dinner crowd his business enjoyed, or what kind of deals he had to strike with the locals to survive in that God-forsaken place.

Jack and I agreed it would be imprudent to stick around until dark to learn the specifics of his security arrangements. It seemed a much longer drive out through the encroaching reed beds than it had been going in, but Jack put the pedal to the metal as I clung to my rifle with a white-knuckled and sweaty grip. We both heaved an enormous sigh of relief when our jeep finally climbed back onto the hardtop and headed for camp.

5
Work Call

Life at the National Training Center was insular and self-absorbed. We had a full schedule and not much access to the outside world until the news of a sudden and dramatic North Vietnamese invasion was radioed to us on 1 April. Although details of the fighting were scanty, we were ordered to cancel the training program and prepare the battalions to be trucked to Saigon the following morning. That evening Colonel Ninh gathered all of our battalion's officers for a special meal that was served on temporary tables set up under some nearby trees. Colonel Ninh provided several bottles of cognac that were soon emptied as a series of toasts were proposed. There was laughing and joking, but also a tough-minded undertone to the evening. Everyone understood we had just received a call to return to combat. While we didn't know the specifics of the events unfolding beyond our horizon, there was a general feeling that this was serious business and we would soon be in the middle of it.

That informal dining-in lasted only a couple of hours, but the event has remained fixed in my memory as a special and poignant experience. There were about thirty officers assigned to the battalion. They were all present that evening, carrying their weapons and wearing their maroon berets. Some were older men with years of combat experience while a few were new to the battalion, replacing others who had been wounded or killed during the previous operation. As I stood among those warriors I recognized how privileged I was to be accepted into their very select club. While I knew something about the human cost of war and fully expected there would be casualties among the group, I was not prepared for the matter-of-fact way they would face and accept death as they led their soldiers on the battlefields of the immediate future.

Early the following morning Jack told me I was being moved to a new job.

The team didn't have enough majors assigned to fill the infantry battalion senior advisor slots, and I was to become the 5th Airborne Battalion's senior advisor. That battalion was one of the three at the National Training Center, and I knew it was not substantially different in size or composition from the others. As we walked across the parade ground to my new assignment Jack told me there were already two Americans serving with the battalion, Lieutenant Winston Cover and a very experienced and impressive platoon sergeant named Ron McCauley. Confident that I was ready for my new job, I thanked Jack for making the recommendation as I prepared to meet the battalion commander, Lieutenant Colonel Nguyen Chi Hieu.

Colonel Hieu was square built for a Vietnamese, and he had served in paratrooper units much of his career. Proud of the fact he had attended the year-long Infantry Career Course at Ft. Benning, Georgia, he was acquainted with American military doctrine and methods and spoke good English. Jack had mentioned he came from a prominent family and his wife was a well-known movie actress. Colonel Hieu was certainly very rank conscious and soon made it obvious that he was not happy with a new senior advisor who was only a captain and not the major he was authorized. After some close questioning concerning my military experience, he seemed willing to accept me, but it was clear his approval came with reservations.

Our initial conversation closed on an incongruous note when Colonel Hieu confided the worst thing he'd seen when he had visited the United States was American women wearing hair curlers when they went shopping. From his perspective as an upper-class and traditional Vietnamese gentleman I understood his distaste for the tackiness he had experienced when visiting Georgia strip malls. In fact I wasn't particularly impressed with that aspect of American life either. At the same time I didn't appreciate him trying to put me in the position of being an apologist for the scruffy side of American society. I knew that the army's program for foreign officers attending service schools in the United States included both military and civilian sponsor-families who provided a variety of contacts in the community. An important part of the program for foreign officers was a year-long schedule of activities giving them a comprehensive picture of American society, so his insistence on stressing the negative the first time we were introduced rubbed me the wrong way.

Although I soon sensed that Colonel Hieu was a bit of a prima donna, I also recognized the importance of establishing some level of rapport since I would be working directly with him for the foreseeable future. Colonel Hieu had been in command for several years and he never asked for and I never presumed to offer tactical advice concerning the employment of the battalion. Nevertheless, I did have a lot of experience adjusting artillery and putting in air strikes, and I was his link to the American fire support that soon became critical to our survival. In the upcoming battles my experience and ability to call for and adjust indirect fires gave me a degree of legitimacy that he eventually came to recognize and depend on. Nonetheless, Colonel Hieu continued to treat me very much as his distinct subordinate, and regardless of the stresses of combat our relationship remained distant. That was a disappointment as I would have enjoyed and appreciated a deeper and more-informed look into Vietnamese society at his level, but I was never invited through that door.

Early the next morning the troops began loading a long convoy of trucks sent down from Saigon. By noon all three battalions had cleared the National Training Center en route to the capital. The advisors threw their gear into jeeps and once on the highway soon caught up with and passed the slower moving trucks. After arriving back at our team building at Tan Son Nhut we were able to get a better picture of why our training program had been canceled, even though our next mission had not yet been clarified.

The North Vietnamese invasion, soon to become known as the Easter Offensive, had kicked off on 30 March with a massive push across the Demilitarized Zone. The attacking enemy divisions included artillery and tank formations and they enjoyed immediate battlefield success. A second big enemy thrust was then initiated much closer to Saigon when major forces attacked out of their Cambodian assembly areas. Those units were also equipped with artillery and tanks and were using National Highway 13, a major high-speed avenue of approach directly into Saigon, as their guide. A third serious incursion had begun to develop in the Central Highlands, about halfway between the other two areas. The South Vietnamese army found itself under growing pressure as the Easter Offensive began to pick up steam.

The Vietnamese Airborne Division's 2nd and 3rd Brigades had both been committed to the expanding battle by the time we arrived in Saigon. That left the division's 1st Brigade, consisting of the three battalions returning from the National Training Center, as the nation's strategic reserve. South Vietnam's national leadership decided to hold our brigade in Saigon until the overall situation could get sorted out. The 5th Airborne Battalion moved onto the grounds of the presidential palace and began a major effort to round up paratroopers on medical leave or otherwise absent. We knew that orders to move were imminent and wanted to go with all the manpower the battalion could generate.

The national leadership took their time deciding where the 1st Airborne Brigade would be committed, and while waiting for orders the advisors ran out of useful things to do. The second evening after arriving back in Saigon several friends invited me to join them in a visit to a venerable institution that, according to them, was available to only the most select clientele. Our destination was the one and only, world famous, Mi Mi's Airborne Bar. That fine establishment was a half-hour ride into the city and located on the ground floor of a multistory corner building near the Saigon River. A large sign over the front door proclaimed its proud name bracketed by a collection of brightly painted Vietnamese, French, and American parachute wings and other airborne badges and mementos. A large bare room was furnished with a long wooden bar, sans mirror, situated along one wall, and a variety of battered tables and chairs casually arranged to accommodate those patrons too weary to hold up the bar. The windows were tall, wide open, and covered with heavy steel screen, admitting a full range of noxious vapors plus an exotic selection of flying bugs wafting up from the river. A variety of naked neon lights, attached to exposed wiring and screwed directly to the sweating walls, bathed the scene in a flickering glare.

Ten or fifteen American sergeants and junior officers were already in residence when we arrived. Definitely of the paratrooper variety, they shared a confident self-assurance and tight haircuts. They were all Special Forces soldiers or advisors to various Vietnamese Ranger or Airborne units, and it soon became clear this was a watering hole reserved for the big boys. There were no fuzzy-cheeked youth hoisting a cold one in Mi Mi's Airborne Bar. The seated patrons had tilted their chairs against the walls and were resting their booted feet on the webbed gear and weapons dumped on the floor. The thirsty souls at the bar had their gear unbuckled and their weapons slung on straps over their shoulders.

Although an initial impression of Mi Mi's clientele might describe them as shabby military casual, on closer inspection it became clear every customer knew exactly how far he had to reach to get his gun. The place looked like a convention of Jump School and Ranger School instructors taking a break from an extended hunting trip. They all observed the kind of alert but nonthreatening and thoughtful demeanor affected by heavily armed men in the presence of others who enjoyed a similar disposition. They had all used their weapons and were respectful of the lethal consequences.

A flock of soiled doves fluttered about, enlivening the atmosphere of the place. The hard-working Vietnamese, Chinese, and Eurasian girls employed by Mi Mi were adept with each new wave of customers, regardless of whether they arrived joyous or mournful. The business was run by a well-preserved Vietnamese madam of indeterminate age who ruled with a gold-toothed grin and an iron hand. Multilingual and well turned out in traditional Viet-

namese dress and heels, she held court from her stool at the end of the bar.
She took great pride in being the latest in a series of managers who answered
to the name Mi Mi.

The old dragon's sense of hospitality and decorum was generally accepted
by her customers, most of whom were willing to respect a piece of local history when they saw one. Hot food could be ordered in from street vendors
and cold beer was in endless supply. A beaded curtain hung over a doorway
at the far end of the room, and Mi Mi proclaimed with enthusiastic conviction that her Airborne Bar was the only place in town where a weary soldier
could still obtain zee oree-sheenal Fransh keeeez.

6
Off to War

On 7 April we learned the 1st Airborne Brigade had been ordered to relieve the garrison defending the province capital of An Loc. The brigade would be built around the three infantry battalions that had been at the National Training Center. It would also include three artillery batteries equipped with 105 mm guns and an engineer detachment with a dozer and backhoe on low-boy trailers. Those units were ordered to assemble, form up in a convoy, and be prepared to depart the next morning at first light.

My map showed the assembly area was located along a portion of High-way 13 in the northwestern outskirts of Saigon. When my driver and I got there we found ourselves right in the middle of a congested urban neighbor-hood. The brigade's assembly area was a mile-long stretch of the urbanized highway. As the evening unfolded I realized the location was actually well chosen as it provided the troops with an opportunity to stretch their legs and get a home-cooked meal before departure. The plan was to initially truck the brigade north on Highway 13 through Ben Cat and Lai Khe toward the town of An Loc. We were told the enemy had cut the highway at some point north of Lai Khe, although the exact location wasn't clear. Our mission was to open the road and reinforce the garrison at An Loc.

When we had been told the battalion was headed into an urban battle I revisited the team supply sergeant and traded in my rifle for a short-barreled 12-gauge shotgun. He also gave me six boxes of oo buckshot shells. My pre-vious experience fighting in cities had convinced me a shotgun was what I wanted, but since I was the only soldier in the battalion carrying one I would only have as many shells as I was willing to carry. Six boxes seemed about right. In fact I didn't expect to use the shotgun much since I'd be in the middle of a battalion of paratroopers; if I ran out of shells I'd be able to take my pick of discarded rifles. The shotgun was an Ithaca Model 37 Feather-light pump gun, an old and trusted friend. Dad and I had gone 50/50 on the same model shotgun years before when I was fifteen and ready to start hunting. It had come equipped with a full-choke barrel and accounted for many a South Dakota rooster pheasant. In fact I still use that dependable old gun when I'm able to get back to stir up the roosters.

My rucksack weighed about eighty pounds with the eight canteens of water, the shotgun shells, and all the C-ration cans that would fit on top of the poncho liner, a couple changes of fatigues, a half dozen pairs of socks, and my shaving gear. I also stuck in several rolls of toilet paper as I had acquired an active distaste for using jungle foliage as a toilette expedient. As it turned out, a case of triple-ply Charmin wouldn't have covered the requirement that eventually arose.

As the evening progressed the units assigned to the brigade began to arrive in the assembly area from their various home compounds. Dozens of trucks, some carrying troops and others pulling water trailers or artillery pieces, shouldered their way up the highway in clouds of diesel and dirt. They pulled off onto the sides of the highway or turned down neighborhood streets to park. Radio jeeps loaded with excitable staff officers shouting into handsets, whip antennas up and waving, raced around the neighborhood.

Laughing housewives began to appear from their kitchens to sell homemade food, served to the troops in family dishes. Soup or white rice with boiled vegetables and chicken or fish were offered from the family pots. The women collected a few coins depending on what food was ordered and then waited patiently for their customers to finish slurping and belching. As soon as the food disappeared the women dunked the used plates, bowls, spoons, and chopsticks in plastic pails of cold water for immediate reuse. Shouting kids selling cold sodas and popsicles out of tin boxes swarmed the unexpected but welcome market of soldiers. More than two thousand troops had appeared in the immediate neighborhood, eating, spitting, chatting with everyone in sight, passing around their newspapers and cigarettes, sleeping in and under the trucks, and wandering around the neighborhood picking their teeth. Operational security was a concept remarkable for its absence.

Everyone in the neighborhood seemed to be personally involved in our departure. The 1st Airborne Brigade finally got itself loaded up and the mile-long convoy shifted into forward gear an hour after daylight on the morning of 8 April. It appeared that all who were supposed to be present actually were. When the 5th Airborne Battalion with its three American advisors departed for war we numbered roughly five hundred soldiers and thirty officers present and prepared for duty.

Our route initially took us through a happy and well–populated country-side whose inhabitants chose to ignore the war going on someplace farther up the road. Cars, trucks, buses, horse carts, motor scooters, and bicycles of every possible description crowded the highway. Their drivers were totally blind to every traffic rule, studiously disregarding the painted lines on the road and all traffic signs as well as their own rear-view mirrors. Drivers seemed to relish playing chicken with all on-coming traffic, and pedestrians of every age wandered across the road as the mood struck them. The favored driving technique was to jockey hard for advantage while honking, weaving, and speeding full-tilt. Our trucks, barreling single file directly down the centerline with air horns blaring, simply ignored every other vehicle on the road. All the traffic took heed and magically parted letting the military convoy knife on through. The one rule that really seemed to matter was size plus determination, and it appeared our convoy held the trump cards.

The brigade spent the night near Lai Khe, and early the next morning our convoy continued north. I began to notice a changing geography as well as a fading social atmosphere in the countryside. The land became bleaker and was not under the same intensive cultivation that existed farther south toward Saigon. Long stretches of scrub brush and tall grass began to appear on both sides of the highway, and planted fields became scarce. Some fifteen miles farther north when we rolled through the village of Chon Thanh, a deserted collection of shacks hugging the highway, there was no traffic on the road and the countryside appeared abandoned and asleep under waves of heat.[1]

A mile north of Chon Thanh the convoy finally ground to a halt in the middle of the shimmering highway and tailgates began to slam down. Soldiers piled out of the trucks as their buddies handed down rucksacks, crew-served weapons, and metal cans of water and ammunition that individuals had been detailed to carry. As quickly as the trucks were unloaded they got turned around and headed back south. The 5th Airborne Battalion was designated to take the lead. Our rifle companies deployed both left and right of the highway and spread out to start the process of searching for the enemy.[2]

The plan was for the three infantry battalions to leapfrog one another up the road. Each morning the first and second battalions in the column would hold in place and the last battalion would leave its position and move forward to become the lead unit for the day. That new lead battalion would then continue north with its rifle companies spread out in the brush on both sides of the highway. The distance they could search from the road was limited by the nature of the terrain and the high grass and brush that stretched to the horizon. The whole maneuver was premised on the belief that the North Vietnamese would position themselves to physically control this southern access to An Loc. We were sure they wouldn't be far off Highway 13.

Each of the infantry battalions had one of the 105 mm artillery batteries attached to provide fire support. The artillery had the range to mass their fires and support all the units in the brigade if required. The guns could also shoot direct fire from their own positions if that should become necessary. The engineers drove their equipment up the highway each afternoon to assist the lead battalion as it dug in for the night. That scheme of maneuver ensured each of the infantry battalions was established in prepared defensive positions before dark.

We encountered the enemy's initial line of resistance later that day, 9 April. In midafternoon the rifle company on the west side of the highway ran into enemy troops occupying a line of newly constructed bunkers. Those fighting positions were actually deep foxholes covered with brush and dirt and impossible to see until close-range shooting began. The paratroopers tried to flank the enemy positions, but without success, so the company commander called for an artillery fire mission. He wanted the artillery to range onto the bunker line with high explosive rounds and then obscure the target with smoke so his men could assault and overrun the enemy. It took several hours to accomplish that task, and then the advancing troops ran into more bunkers located on both sides of the road. The attacking rifle companies conducted another assault under cover of artillery fire and smoke. Forward movement was finally halted about six o'clock because the battalion needed to consolidate and establish its defensive position for the night. The 5th Airborne Battalion had cleared over a mile of road that day and was ready for a fresh battalion to continue the advance the following morning.

We moved into a position still under construction on the east side of Highway 13, immediately next to the road. The engineers had appeared and were working as the rifle companies arrived out of the brush. About fifty yards across, the position was in the shape of a square. The dozer was busily pushing earth out from the middle to build a berm roughly five feet high around the perimeter. Each company was assigned a side and the troops dug individual positions into the dirt for protection.

The engineers also buried a modified steel shipping container in the center of the square. The container was equipped with radios on shelves and antennas attached to the top, providing a protected and ready-made command post. The artillery pieces were being pushed into dozed-out pits inside the square, positioned so they could provide all-around support. As the rifle com-

panies arrived the artillery began firing to the north at likely enemy locations. It was a compact but business-like setup.

Just before dark two of the brigade's trucks arrived with a supply of small
arms ammunition, grenades, M-72 Light Anti-Tank Weapons (LAWs), and
food for the battalion. One of the trucks was pulling a water trailer, which
was especially welcome. We needed the ammunition, too, particularly the
LAWs, a one-shot, shoulder-fired rocket very effective for busting bunkers.
Considering the nature of the fighting that day we knew more bunkers would
be uncovered as the brigade moved forward. We had taken casualties during the day and several dead tied into their plastic ponchos and a half dozen
wounded paratroopers were in the trucks when they departed. The artillery
battery also received several pallets of ammunition as the sun was setting.
Their supply was delivered in nylon slings suspended under a heavy-lift helicopter, and it arrived with the hurricane of dust and grit that was always part
of a Chinook helicopter hovering over a patch of raw dirt.

We expected some action that night considering the proximity of the
enemy. Because we were the battalion farthest up the road toward An Loc,
we anticipated being the first unit to receive a North Vietnamese ground attack. Long before it got dark I made sure my communications were good with
the American Air Force forward air controller (FAC) loitering in his little airplane high overhead.

The short-range FM radios used by troops on the ground were battery
powered and carried by soldiers. Fighter planes were equipped with high-
powered UHF and VHF radios that were much too heavy to carry. The FAC
was able to accomplish his coordination task because his airplane was equipped
with all three types. That allowed him to talk to and coordinate everyone
who was involved in close air support missions. The FAC's airplane also carried under-wing pods of smoke rockets used to mark ground targets. Without
those smoke markers, fast-moving fighter pilots had difficulty pinpointing
exact enemy locations. That degree of precision bombing was very important
to ground troops, particularly when the targets were close. The communications link provided by the FAC was not required when army Cobra helicopters or the big Air Force multiengine gunships were providing fire support.
Those aircraft carried FM radios so troops on the ground could talk to them
and adjust their fires directly.

About an hour after dark the enemy began to search for our location with
mortars. Although the rounds landed outside our defensive square we did
take some accurate small-arms fire. An enemy recoilless rifle also began to
shoot at our position from the west, across the highway. Probably a Chinese

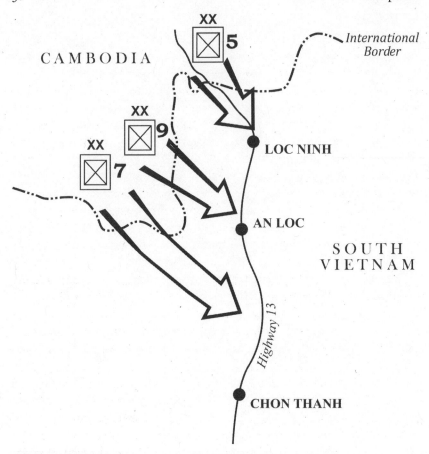

2. This graphic depicts the general axis of advance for the three North Vietnamese army divisions attacking out of Cambodia toward Saigon.

57 mm weapon, sometimes called a reckless rifle by the troops because of the terrific back blast that helped mark its location, it could be man-handled across country by its crew. It had a very fast muzzle velocity and it was accurate and deadly. The high-explosive shell seemed to arrive with the sound of the weapon being fired. There was little or no time to duck when someone shot a reckless rifle in your direction.

That was the first time since being assigned to Team 162 that I'd been able to put in an air strike, and I gave the FAC a call on my radio. He was soon circling over our position. Although the FAC was looking down onto our stretch of highway from about two thousand feet he wasn't able to see the recoilless rifle's muzzle flash or back blast. When he told me he was having trouble identifying the target I turned on a strobe light inside the berm closest to the highway. The FAC immediately saw my flashing light and could clearly see the north-south highway in the moonlight, so I was confident he knew exactly where the 5th Airborne Battalion was located.

I directed him to put in an air strike immediately across the road to the west of my position. The recoilless rifle was about a hundred and fifty yards from the road, and when the FAC told me the fighters were loaded with napalm I was sure we'd put the recoilless rifle crew and everyone else in the vicinity out of business. I requested that the fighters approach the target from south to north, flying parallel to and up the west side of the highway. I wanted to be absolutely certain there was no chance any of the napalm could splash toward friendly troops. The FAC told me the fighters were a pair of U.S. Air Force A-1 Skyraiders and confirmed that the pilots could identify the highway and that they also had a good fix on my strobe light. I was happy to hear a flight of Skyraiders would be putting in the strike. They were older propeller-driven fighters known for their durability and precision. I didn't want to miss either the gun crew or any enemy infantry that might be supporting them.

The FAC fired a rocket to confirm the enemy's location, and when the fighters were inbound I informed Colonel Hieu and he ordered the troops to get down. And then the A-1s came barreling out of the night sky, one behind the other. There were a couple of terrific explosions and a gigantic flash of fire that looked like the napalm had been delivered right into the highway ditch. In fact it was at least a hundred yards to the west of the road, but near enough for everyone to feel the heat.

The battalion commander must have thought he had been given a peek through the very gates of hell because he dashed over to where I was on the berm, waving his arms and shouting for me to stop the strike. I didn't intend to stop anything because I knew the enemy gun crew was not alone, and I directed the FAC to follow up with another load of fire and damnation. I told him to put the next load just to the west of where the first air strike had gone in so we would catch any North Vietnamese trying to scurry out of the way. He followed my directions to the letter and the next strike went in with a bang and another tremendous ball of fire. That run was followed by several more spectacular displays of fighter planes roaring out of the night sky accompanied by searing blasts of napalm that set the countryside on fire. Colonel Hieu stood frozen mute in amazement, and the reckless rifle became equally silent.

7
Visiting Brass

The paratroopers of the 8th Airborne Battalion began moving past our position at first light the following morning, well spread out on both sides of the highway as they started their search for the enemy's next line of bunkers. They were very aware of the engagements we had fought the previous day, and we gave them our LAWs as they moved past. Busting bunkers was sure to be on their agenda and we expected to get another supply before the day was over. The heavily loaded paratroopers were moving with purpose, but with caution, as they intended to find the enemy without being surprised in the process.

The night had been clear with a star-filled sky, but as the sun rose higher the day turned blistering hot. Once the sun had broken the horizon the companies sent patrols into the surrounding brush. Soldiers remaining in our position began building innovative sunshades by propping up ponchos, scraps of plastic sheeting, and pieces of cardboard from C-ration boxes. The inside of the berm took on the appearance of a hobo's camp as the troops tried to escape the sun's direct effects. The temperature climbed into the high 90s from midmorning until late afternoon, and the sun bore down into our raw dirt position hour after hour. A slight breeze provided dust but no cooling effect, and the time dragged.

The enemy fired eight or ten mortar rounds that hit about a hundred yards up the highway. When they began to impact I quickly retreated to the stifling underground command post as there was no telling when some of them might explode inside the position. I could listen to the tactical radios in the underground shelter, but when it was quiet I preferred to sit in the shade of my jeep, which was also equipped with radios. It was important for me to keep up with the other battalion's activities and by switching frequencies I could listen to artillery fire missions and calls to the FAC for tactical air strikes. Red dust and the stink of burned powder drifted across the ground when the artillery battery went into action. Helicopter gunships and tactical fighters hit targets farther up the road periodically throughout the day. It was a slow business and I had little to do but monitor the overall situation as I stewed in my own sweat, drank warm canteen water, listened to the radios, and swatted at flies. The joys of Mi Mi's Airborne Bar were fast becoming a fading memory.

In midafternoon the tedium was suddenly broken by a jeep that came flying off the highway. It slid to a stop in an annoying cloud of dust and out jumped an aging but slim and energetic American wearing a steel helmet that sported the two stars of a major general. He also had an oversized pearl-handled pistol strapped around the waist of his starched jungle fatigues. Considering that he was normally catered to in a comfortable villa, his great big pistol struck me as a silly kind of affectation. It's possible my attitude was influenced by the fact I didn't have one for myself—either a villa or a great big shiny pistol. At any rate the man was certainly a bundle of energy as he waved his arms and demanded to know what was going on, who was doing it, where it was happening, how well it was being done, and what kinds of problems needed his attention. It turned out he was Major General James Hollingsworth, the commanding general of the Third Regional Assistance Command, also known as TRAC.[1] An Loc and the operation to reopen Highway 13 were well within his area of responsibility and the TRAC commanding general had arrived to get a personal feel for the progress of the battle.

General Hollingsworth's jeep was closely followed by several civilian cars that also pulled into the battalion position. The cars were full of American media people from Saigon, tastefully attired in the Abercrombie & Fitch style of pseudo-military uniform featuring numerous pockets, straps, and buckles. They affected the hotel barfly, tropical-casual look I'd seen displayed throughout Southeast Asia. Cameras and notebooks were on instant display as they climbed out of their cars. It appeared the media had been chasing the general up Highway 13 and had finally cornered him. They quickly gathered around in a tight cluster and started clamoring. In response to the very first barrage of questions, General Hollingsworth turned on his audience and launched into a fantastic harangue. He refused to answer their demands, but cut loose with a tirade built around damning the communist enemy to an everlasting and painful level of Hades.

The general described a special kind of profane punishment he intended for those miscreants causing the current troubles. He was particularly incensed by how the North Vietnamese were blocking Highway 13. In his view they had provided him with a great opportunity. He intended to take full advantage of their impertinence by administering a beating that he described in a dramatically obscene and blood-curdling fashion. The verbal fireworks went on for some time, heavily flavored with the most creative, graphic, and instructive profanity I had enjoyed in years. It soon became clear that General Hollingsworth didn't intend to answer any questions and he also didn't intend to be quoted by the aggressive media personalities.

The reporters finally gave up trying to wring a direct response out of him, and they switched tactics when one of them asked if they could quote his comments verbatim. Laughing, the answer was you #%@*&$! right you can. There was no shade available for the journalists, and they didn't seem to care for either the blazing heat or the unmistakable implications of the battle being conducted farther up the highway. An air strike was going in a quarter mile from where we were standing, and the artillery in our position had begun to fire. As soon as it became clear the impromptu press conference wasn't going to produce anything quotable, the journalists climbed back into their cars and sped back down the highway toward the comforts of an air-conditioned Saigon.

Once they disappeared down the road General Hollingsworth switched personas and became the engaging and professional leader that marked him as a real warrior. He spent half an hour with the battalion. First he climbed down into the underground command post and provided an overview of the developing war. He asked a series of questions that were both thoughtful and insightful, wanting to know how the battalion was organized and deployed. He asked about our recent fighting and had questions concerning equipment and supply problems. The availability and effectiveness of fire support was a particular interest. He then grabbed me and we walked part of the berm. The Vietnamese paratroopers on the line were surprised to have an American major general suddenly appear in their midst. Once they recognized his rank they immediately jumped up and saluted, shouting an enthusiastic welcome. General Hollingsworth was impressed by their alertness and spontaneous response to his arrival; he obviously understood and loved being with combat soldiers.

That was the only time I saw General Hollingsworth, although as the battle progressed I talked to him a number of times by radio, particularly after the brigade was pulled away from the Highway 13 mission and airlifted to An Loc. During that later phase of the battle General Hollingsworth was often orbiting over the besieged garrison in his helicopter. He seemed to be there when the fighting was the heaviest, encouraging and guiding, pumping up and promising the air support that was essential to survive in that terrible place. He was the man who kept the show together. He ensured that the massive volume of air power essential for the survival of An Loc's garrison kept coming and that it was delivered when and where it was most needed.

I am absolutely sure General Hollingsworth made the difference between life and death for me personally. I, and every other American advisor I knew, respected and loved him. In my experience South Vietnamese officers also saw him as an important leader in the fight. At the same time some of them might have viewed him and what he symbolized with a tinge of resentment. The Easter Offensive was fast becoming a test of the South Vietnamese army's ability to defend the country, and Colonel Hieu, as an example, was coming to the embarrassing realization that without continuing American support South Vietnam might just get plowed under.

The following day we were visited by a Vietnamese colonel who unexpectedly flew in to check on the situation. He was doing a commander's reconnaissance for an armor unit that was en route to help open the highway and he arrived with a bit of unexpected flair. Our first clue that he wanted to drop by was when his helicopter startled everyone by roaring low across our position before swinging back to land in the grass beside the berm.

The colonel, whose name I later learned was Truong Huu Duc, wasn't much more than five feet tall.[2] He was wearing a steel helmet with the straps pulled tight and buckled under his chin, and his flack vest was buttoned up to his neck. He obviously wasn't willing to make any concessions to the midday heat where his personal security was concerned. He jumped out of his helicopter wearing a pistol in a shoulder holster and the kind of tanker's boots that include multiple straps and buckles around the ankles. A pair of staff officers had to trot to keep up as he quick-timed into the battalion's position on bandy legs, grinning through a bristling mustache and saluting left and right. He looked like a jolly little gentleman, and he spent only a few minutes with the battalion commander down in the command post before charging back to his aircraft.

The helicopter cranked up as the colonel climbed aboard and got strapped into a seat next to one of the door gunners, and then it quickly lifted off in a full-throated roar and a swirl of dirt and exhaust. The aircraft was about a hundred yards out and climbing when a heavy machine gun began to fire from outside the berm. I watched the helicopter immediately twist back and come to a skidding, smoking halt near where it had just taken off. An enemy .51-caliber machine-gun crew had worked in close to our position and remained undetected in the tall grass until they opened up when the helicopter flew across them.

The little colonel was hanging in his seat straps, covered in blood. A slug had caught him under the chin and ripped through his head and out the top of his steel helmet, blowing blood and brains all over the inside of the crew compartment. No one else in the helicopter had been hit, but other rounds had damaged parts of the aircraft and ripped several holes through the main rotor blades. Our battalion doctor and his medics wrapped the little colonel in a plastic poncho and tied him up tight with parachute cord while the aircraft crew called for another helicopter to come retrieve them.

The enemy machine-gun crew had gotten established outside 53 Company's portion of the berm, and the company commander sent a platoon out to kill them. The soldiers attacked directly into the grass and weren't gone long before a burst of automatic fire and several grenade blasts marked their progress. The paratroopers were back in their fighting positions with the heavy machine gun in tow before the colonel's poncho-wrapped body had been loaded on the replacement aircraft for his final flight home.

Later that evening I was listening to an American advisor with the 8th Airborne Battalion farther up the road as he was talking to a FAC. The sun had dropped below the horizon and they were coordinating an air strike. And then the FAC's low-key, professional demeanor seemed to slip. He could see a big area of muzzle flashes right along the highway, and he'd suddenly realized a large group of people were shooting at him. That's when his voice went up a couple of octaves as he shouted there must be at least a regiment shooting right at him, trying to knock him out of the sky. The FAC seemed to take it personally and repeated his discovery several times with greater and greater conviction. He insisted there were thousands of them, all shooting at him with malicious intent. As the advisor on the ground paused to consider the implications of that sobering message, I joined the conversation. I said it sounded like he had a good target and it was time to hit it with everything he could get his hands on before the shooters could get away. He did.

The FAC's excitement told me there were a lot more North Vietnamese headed my way, although at that point I didn't suspect a full division of approximately 9,000 men had the mission of cutting the highway. Their task was to ensure the South Vietnamese defenders in An Loc could not receive any overland support. If I'd known there were that many of the enemy between me and the brigade objective I'd have become more persistent with my Acts of Contrition. I did begin to appreciate, however, that the situation must be getting grim for the South Vietnamese soldiers already surrounded in the city.

In fact I and everyone else in the brigade would soon find out just how difficult it had actually become in that isolated place. We would learn that while some of the survivors from earlier battles near the Cambodian border had been able to reach An Loc, major units of the North Vietnamese army had also arrived. The first shelling of the city had begun on 5 April, and four days later, the same day we first engaged the enemy along Highway 13, North Vietnamese infantry started probing the garrison's defenses. On the thirteenth a massive artillery barrage had preceded major enemy ground attacks supported by tanks and the South Vietnamese defenders were forced to consolidate in the southern half of the city. That was the embattled garrison we would eventually join.

It wasn't until much later that I was able to gain a better understanding of the forces engaged in the battle for An Loc. Appendix 1 provides a comprehensive listing of both enemy and friendly units that were deployed during the course of that epic struggle.

8
A Media Event

When a dusty Buick pulled off the highway and a pudgy and rumpled American in his mid-fifties hoisted himself out, I knew I was looking at another kind of veteran. The gentleman's clothes looked like they'd been slept in and a battered straw hat was pushed back on his head. Once my visitor got his bearings he strolled over to where I was sitting in my jeep and showed me his press card. It was midday, the sun was bearing down, and I was trying to stay cool without much success. I invited this slightly frowzy representative of the fourth estate to join me. As soon as he got settled in the other front seat of the jeep he produced a hip flask and offered me a pull. I appreciated the thought but it was a bit too early in the day for me to be drinking neat whisky out of a hot flask. Neither the time of day nor the temperature of the beverage seemed to slow him down, and as he drained the flask we discussed the state of the world and the ongoing battles to clear the enemy roadblocks.

My new friend from the press told me that his car had been shot at on the drive up from Saigon. Both he and his Vietnamese driver thought they had seen soldiers in khaki uniforms and sun helmets crouching in the brush along the highway south of Chon Thanh, toward Lai Khe. He was sure they were North Vietnamese and he was concerned about getting back to Saigon that afternoon. That was the first I'd heard the enemy might already be farther south on Highway 13 and decided maybe he had a good reason to empty his flask after all.

As subsequent events were to demonstrate, he had probably seen a North Vietnamese reconnaissance team well in advance of major enemy units moving in behind us. Once I'd established an encrypted link with advisors at the brigade's base camp at Lai Khe, I passed on the reporter's account of the enemy troops he had seen. I also put in an order for water and ammunition the battalion needed.

Several months later I learned that my press friend's account of our conversation had been printed as a front-page article in the 16 April 1972 issue of *Pacific Stars & Stripes*. It had also been picked up by a number of other newspapers in the United States and several friends sent me copies. It was run under Hugh Mulligan's byline and included the following uplifting, if somewhat creative and wide-ranging, narrative:

"What's wrong with this girl?" asked Captain Mike McDermott, holding up a Pacific Stars & Stripes that showed Raquel Welch in fulsome cleavage at the Academy Awards ceremony. He was hard to hear over the blam-blam of howitzers firing at an enemy machinegun somewhere nearby in the jungle scrubs. McDermott, from Highmore, S.D., squatted at a field telephone in the corrugated sewer pipe serving as his front line command post on Highway 13, Vietnam's Thunder Road.

A four-year man in the Nam, having extended twice on previous tours with the 101st Airborne, the captain took issue with a visitor (in fact Mulligan) who called Highway 13 "interesting." "That's rear echelon talk," he corrected between telephone squawks telling why he couldn't get more air strikes and what had become of the water he ordered yesterday for his men. "It's not interesting. It's dangerous."

Mulligan's article went on to recount the adventures of his trip up from Saigon. He then reviewed a short history of the major battles previously fought along that stretch of the highway before returning to our discussion. "Now no one knows what will happen along Thunder Road, least of all the men fighting there. 'All I know is what's happening 100 yards in front of me, and that ain't good,'" said McDermott.

After I eventually got back to the United States my mother, who was the county librarian as well as a retired rural schoolteacher, asked if I really used the bad grammar quoted in the article. I assured her the author probably inserted the questionable verbiage to somehow make our soldierly conversation more authentic. Perhaps he thought it might be a symbol of manly military-media bonding. Or maybe that's what Mulligan actually thought he'd heard as he struggled with the high-octane haze he'd been working on in the midday heat. At any rate, the article, which can be read at Appendix 2, was my only confirmation that my disheveled friend had made it back to Saigon without encountering serious problems along the road. At the time, however, neither I nor anyone else in the 1st Airborne Brigade was looking in the direction of his departure. We were faced north toward An Loc, a destination that demanded our full and undivided attention.

9
Hitting the Wall

The day the 5th Airborne Battalion locked horns with the enemy's first line of resistance marked the beginning of a series of battles that became more deadly as we pressed the attack. The 1st Airborne Brigade continued to spearhead the South Vietnamese army's effort to open Highway 13 by rotating one battalion up front while the other two prepared to move forward in their turn. That tactic became our modus operandi. The trailing battalions were fully employed patrolling the cleared portions of the road and securing the brigade's artillery, which was firing primarily in support of the lead battalion. Replacement soldiers arrived on the supply trucks from Saigon each day and the dead and wounded were evacuated when the trucks returned to the city. Even though our foxhole strength remained stable, the farther we pushed up the road the more North Vietnamese we encountered. New enemy units were arriving on the battlefield from their sanctuaries in Cambodia, and with each passing day the ratios got worse for us.

A negative event that seemed to symbolize my relationship with the battalion commander occurred during those days of combat along the highway. Late one morning I was standing beside my radio jeep, talking to the overhead FAC as we set up an air strike, when Colonel Hieu walked over. He said he wanted to put in the strike and reached for the handset. Based on his English language skills and experience I was sure he could do it and told the FAC the battalion commander was going to provide the request. I handed Colonel Hieu the handset and he began to talk, and that's when things started getting difficult. His directions were wandering, confusing, and repetitious. When he paused to take a breath, the FAC asked for clarification. Colonel Hieu was visibly upset when he realized his directions weren't being understood. He launched into another long and confusing transmission, accompanied by much arm waving. The FAC was also struggling.

Colonel Hieu glanced at me, then turned his back and gave it another effort. His directions weren't getting through and he was angry and embarrassed. The FAC was also getting frustrated because aircraft time on station was a critical factor in his business. When he said he wanted to talk to the American the handset got shoved back in my direction. I put in the air strike and waited a bit before going to find the steaming battalion commander. I told him the FAC worked from a standardized format and wouldn't put in an air strike when he wasn't sure about the target. Colonel Hieu wasn't buying my explanation, and it soon became clear the most serious aspect of the incident was his bruised dignity. My feelings about the whole event solidified a day or so later when I offered Colonel Hieu a written format for practicing air strike requests with the FAC. He refused to discuss it. I knew it would have been to his advantage to learn that process, especially when the possibility of an untoward turn of fate could have left him without an American to depend on.

Additional South Vietnamese infantry units were being brought up from the delta and were digging in immediately to our rear. It soon looked like several regiments had arrived with thousands of soldiers entrenching both east and west of the highway. While there were a lot of friendly troops behind us, the airborne battalions continued to rotate to the front as we attacked north into stronger and stronger enemy positions. Progress was slow and painful. It eventually became clear to the leadership in Saigon that Highway 13 would not be secured any time soon by attacking on a one-battalion front, no matter how tough and dedicated those paratroopers might be. As the enemy's resistance became stronger, the airborne brigade's progress began to stall.

South Vietnam's national leadership decided to tip the scales by bringing in a bigger hammer. I was told part of an armored cavalry squadron augmented by an ad hoc outfit from the South Vietnamese Armor Training School was joining the fight. This was the armor unit the ill-fated Colonel Duc had been doing the reconnaissance for. Deploying a unit that included resources from the training base meant the last reserves of armor were being committed. It looked as though the South Vietnamese army was scraping the bottom of the barrel to reopen Highway 13.

The composite armor unit arrived on a day when I was operating out of a defensive position in the middle of the brigade column. The 8th Airborne Battalion was once again ahead of us, a half mile farther up the road, and they were engaged in a knock-down slugfest with dug-in North Vietnamese infantry. Six or eight M-48 tanks, accompanied by two armored personnel carriers rigged as command and control tracks, came roaring up the highway from the south and ground to a halt in a cloud of swirling dust and diesel exhaust. Two of the tanks and the two tracks drove right inside our position while the rest of the tanks parked and idled along the highway. The rear ramp on one of the tracks came down, and a Vietnamese officer climbed out to confer with the battalion commander. After a few minutes the armor officer jumped back into his track and the ramp went back up. The armor vehicles in our position continued to sit there, but the tanks outside on the highway headed north toward the ongoing fight.

A small group of soldiers joined me on the berm to watch the unfolding drama. Two of the advancing tanks stayed on the shoulders of the hard-topped road and the rest deployed into the high grass and brush on both sides of the highway as they approached the ongoing fight. They hardly slowed down as they went through our sister battalion's positions and into the enemy's bunker line. The paratroopers immediately jumped up and followed behind them, and the enemy was overwhelmed in very short order. The attack was carried out with virtually no coordination between the tanks and the 8th Airborne Battalion, but the shock effect of the armor and the aggressiveness of the paratroopers ensured the majority of the North Vietnamese were killed in their bunkers. The soldiers cleaned up their new position and called the engineers forward with their dozer and backhoe to bury the enemy dead and scrape out a new defensive position.

The success of the afternoon's battle emboldened the armor commander, and his unit prepared to continue up the highway toward An Loc with a night attack. The intent was to break through any roadblocks that might be encountered and charge on into the provincial capital some fifteen miles farther north. The armor unit also called forward a half dozen of their trucks that had been waiting back down the road. There were several fuel tankers in the convoy and the rest of the trucks were loaded with ammo and troops. The armor vehicles in our position moved onto the highway and escorted the trucks forward to join the tanks that were waiting for them. It was well after dark when all the tanks and tracks had been refueled and rearmed, and that was when the fireworks really started.

The whole armor column moved past the 8th Airborne Battalion's position and started north up the highway with all their lights off. The blacked-out vehicles were in a single column with the trucks interspersed among the tanks and tracks as they took off into the night. They hadn't gone a half mile when they ran into a major problem.

It started when the lead tanks blundered into the middle of a column of enemy infantry crossing the road. Instead of being intimidated by the tanks, the North Vietnamese folded back onto the road and hundreds of enemy soldiers were suddenly swarming all over the convoy. Rather than attempt to accelerate through the blazing firefight and continue up the highway, the armor column got bogged down.

The tanks and tracks buttoned up in an effort to defend themselves when everyone in the column opened fire. Several of the tanks were equipped with search lights that got switched on. The trucks also turned on their lights in an effort to see the enemy. Some of the tanks loaded main gun beehive rounds, which are giant shotgun shells, and blasted into the dark. In several cases they intentionally fired at other tanks to clear off the crowds of enemy climbing everywhere. The fuel and ammo trucks began to explode and burn. Within ten minutes the entire column had become a gaggle of vehicles strung out on the highway, frantically trying to extricate themselves from a surging mass of tenacious enemy soldiers. Confusion reigned supreme. Command and control was totally and irrevocably lost. Hopes of roaring up the road to An Loc were shelved.

That meeting engagement took place less than a mile from my position. The light show was spectacular with great balls of fire and enormous explosions throwing showers of fiery sparks high into the sky. Streams of red and green tracers sliced across the horizon and arced in every direction. I listened as the 8th Airborne Battalion advisors worked with the FAC to adjust air strikes into the areas surrounding the armor column. All the artillery within range was firing at suspected enemy positions. Illumination rounds were popping over the battle site and the whole countryside was a shifting mix of stark magnesium glare and black shadows as the high-intensity flares swung under their parachutes. The armor vehicles finally broke loose and came thundering back down the highway. They passed our sister battalion's position without slowing down and came to a stop where they had initially started, in and around my position. All the fuel and ammo trucks had been destroyed. The only South Vietnamese troops who survived were the few clinging frantically to the tops of the armor vehicles as they came roaring out of the night.

Late the next morning a pair of five-ton flatbed trucks arrived from Saigon. Their mission was to accompany the armor back up the highway to the scene of the previous night's battle and recover the South Vietnamese dead. It took them several hours, but once their gruesome task was completed the armor stopped on the road near my position. The two trucks pulled inside the berm so the drivers could cover their grisly burdens with tarps before heading back south. Several dozen dead men had been thrown onto each of the trucks.

They were piled in tangled heaps, rigid and stiff with their clawed hands curled up over their faces. Most of the bodies were badly burned and some

3. Airborne artillery providing fire support for troops in combat. Photo courtesy of Pham, vnafmamn.

were charred beyond recognition. It was very hot in the direct sun and the sickening stench was like an opaque haze around the trucks. Clouds of flies buzzed everywhere. A group of paratroopers helped the drivers get canvas covers tied down over the dead. They also tied a South Vietnamese flag across the top of each load. A thin sheet of blood and goo washed off the steel truck beds as the two vehicles pulled out onto the highway and headed south to Saigon.

North Vietnamese commanders had anticipated Saigon's attempt to re-open Highway 13 and elements of several enemy regiments were already in place to block any relief effort. The armor unit's fight on the highway had been a setback, and certainly put the quietus to any hopes of reinforcing the troops in An Loc quickly. The fight was costly for the enemy as well, but the North Vietnamese would have seen the incident very differently. They were undoubtedly pleased that a potential link-up with the An Loc garrison had been foiled, and in fact were moving more troops into position to replace their losses while they further strengthened their position on the battlefield.

Those new enemy units quickly made their presence felt, and by the next morning our sister battalion a half mile north of us was under serious and growing pressure. Accurate mortar and rocket fire was slamming into their position and enemy troops were maneuvering in the brush and tall grass to get closer. The defending paratroopers were supported by air strikes and all the friendly artillery within range, and they were fighting hard to defend themselves. As the morning wore on it became more and more evident the soldiers of that battalion were being fixed in their position and forced to fight for their lives. Enemy small arms and mortar fire also began to impact in and around our position. As that incoming fire intensified it became clear the enemy's forces were large enough to conduct a coordinated attack to keep us in place while they prepared to overwhelm the battalion just up the road. The situation was getting grim.

About noon that day, 14 April, I learned the brigade had received new orders. We were going to conduct an assault by helicopter directly into An Loc to reinforce the city's defenders. Instead of attacking up the highway to support our beleaguered comrades, the whole brigade was ordered to conduct a fighting withdrawal back down the highway and hand off the battle to the units dug in behind us. Once that task was accomplished, we would secure a landing zone south of Chon Thanh for the upcoming air assault. We were going to extract ourselves from one battlefield to be inserted into another using the speed and surprise provided by helicopters. The plan sounded good; doing it was going to be a complicated and chancy project.

10

Shifting Gears

With the armor unit's debacle the enemy must have concluded they had a hammerlock on the 8th Airborne Battalion. The paratrooper's were being pounded with mortar and rocket fire and enemy infantry was in the process of tightening a noose around their position. I'd been monitoring the radios from our dug-in command post when the hard-pressed paratroopers were ordered to disengage from the enemy and fight their way back down Highway 13. To accomplish that mission they would have to surprise the enemy and make their move using all the firepower available.

The first indication I had that our fellow paratroopers were actually withdrawing was when their artillery trucks appeared bouncing down the road ditch, with their guns in tow. They were closely followed by several jeeps loaded with the command group and advisors. The trucks and jeeps were all carrying dead and wounded and using the roadbed for cover from the enemy's small-arms fire. Close behind the vehicles a rifle company of about a hundred men came jogging down the ditch. They were well spread out and covered with sweat. Helmets bouncing and bent forward under their rucksacks and weapons, they looked exhausted but quickly moved on past my position.

A second and then a third company followed close behind. Finally the battalion's rear guard came into view, shooting and running, shooting and running. The paratroopers had been able to surprise the enemy by unexpectedly attacking out of their defensive position. Their sudden aggressiveness had been accompanied by all the tactical air support and artillery fire available. They had kicked off their move with a massive barrage including dozens of smoke rounds to mask their attack, which had been conducted straight south, back down the highway. The paratroopers had outdistanced most of the enemy, but a lot of small-arms fire followed them as the last soldiers moved past my position.

The enemy was pressing the departing paratroopers, and several of the more careless North Vietnamese were killed by soldiers standing near me who nailed them from the top of our berm. Once the 8th Airborne Battalion had moved past our position, the advancing enemy shifted their attention to us. Everyone standing on the berm was soon forced to take cover. The enemy mortars firing at the recently evacuated position up the road began to shift their fires. Within an hour the intensity of incoming rounds increased dramatically and began to impact with greater accuracy. We were soon under a combined infantry and indirect fire attack as the enemy got coordinated. I contacted the FAC and began putting in air strikes as quickly as aircraft came on station. My focus was primarily on those mortars and I adjusted air strikes to the north and into the brush on both sides of the highway.

The troops in my position were dug into the earthen berm around the perimeter, and they were finding more and more targets. The armor unit's two tracks and several of their tanks were still idling inside the position, although the other tanks had departed back down the highway. Our artillery pieces were partially protected in gun pits and were all firing nonstop. Although we had not yet been ordered to disengage and follow our sister battalion south, I was sure we would soon be told to move. I gave Lieutenant Cover and Sergeant McCauley a heads-up and instructed my driver to get the jeep closer to the highway at the far corner of the position.

I was down inside the buried command post talking to the overhead FAC when a pair of civilians unexpectedly stuck their heads through the door. A man and a woman, French reporters, dressed in olive drab chic and draped with cameras and attitude, demanded to know the latest developments in no uncertain terms. I decided to take advantage of an opportunity to escape the stifling bunker for a few minutes, despite their supercilious attitude. The battalion executive officer, a major, joined me as I climbed outside to talk to them. I noticed a third Frenchman standing near their car, which was parked close to one of the tanks.

We had just gathered beside the idling tank when three mortar rounds suddenly slammed into the ground on the far side of the vehicle. Those rounds arrived with no warning and went off with a big bang. Dirt and steel shrapnel flew and smoke and dust boiled up. The first three rounds were immediately followed by three more. One exploded directly on top of the armored personnel carrier parked closest to us, about ten yards from where we were standing. Shrapnel and sparks flew in every direction, but over our heads.

The Vietnamese major and I glanced at each other, knowing it was too late to duck, but the three French journalists were all hugging the ground. They were flattened out next to the tank's treads when that forty-ton monster was unexpectedly thrown into gear and lurched backward, away from the smoking track. The journalists leaped up and without so much as a single adieu scrambled into their car and tore down the road toward Saigon. They departed in real haste, although one did leave a spreading puddle in the dirt next to where the tank had been parked.

The executive officer and I tried to get the damaged track's back hatch open, but it was jammed tight. The vehicle was burning and we had to back away when ammo started to cook off. None of the Vietnamese in the burning track were able to get out. Eventually the rubber pads on the treads caught fire and the fuel went up with a roar. The fire became extremely hot and some of the aluminum began to melt and drip onto the ground. Oily black smoke rose straight up into a clear sky for a thousand feet, and the major and I ran for the underground bunker as more mortar rounds arrived. The other track and the tanks pulled out onto the highway and drove south toward Chon Thanh to join their comrades.

Sometime later the major and I again climbed outside the sweltering steel bunker to get a breath of fresh air. Small-arms rounds and pieces of mortar shrapnel whined across the position, so we hunkered down close to the entrance as we assessed the situation. Suddenly the major grunted and sat down in the dirt. He was bent over and gripping his right hand, which began to spurt blood. A piece of shrapnel had clipped off part of his hand to include the thumb. I pulled him down into the bunker and helped a medic tourniquet his arm and bandage his hand. He was going into shock as we bundled him into a jeep for the trip south. Still wearing his steel helmet and armored vest, which had become slick with blood, he gave me a left-handed salute as the driver threw the jeep into gear.

I was back down inside the command bunker, sweating and talking to the overhead FAC, when an absolutely tremendous, bone-bending explosion went off. It felt as though the whole bunker had been slammed really hard. The generator stopped, the lights went out, and the radios went dead. Colonel Hieu ordered everyone out although we didn't know what had actually happened. It felt like the biggest cannon shell or rocket in the world had gone off right on top of us. The first thing I sensed when I scrambled out was that the whole interior of the defensive position was engulfed in dust and smoke. Through the turmoil I saw several 105 mm rounds lying loose on the ground. Then several more came spinning through the air and thumped down nearby. That was when I realized an enemy rocket or mortar shell had hit a pallet of artillery ammunition, causing some of the rounds to explode and throwing the rest all over the position. There was a lot of confusion in the artillery gun pits, but the surviving members of the gun crews were already hooking their guns to the trucks. It was obvious they were pulling out. Troops on the berm were firing across the top of the dirt wall at enemy infantry pressing in from the north and east. The 105 mm rounds continued to cook off inside the position, throwing clouds of dirt and chunks of shrapnel in every direction.

My driver suddenly appeared out of the dust and smoke to retrieve me. He had parked the jeep near the road before running back to make sure I knew it was time to leave. I told him I would join him in a minute and jumped back down into the bunker to find the battalion commander. He was busy issuing orders to the company commanders, and it was clear the battalion was preparing to move. My personal gear was in my jeep, so I grabbed a backpack radio and my shotgun and left the bunker. I had to run across the open center of the position to get to my jeep, and was about halfway there and running hard when I suddenly saw an artillery shell lying directly in my path. It was so close that I just high-stepped right across without slowing down. The round was smoking from both the nose and the butt end and it looked terrifying. For just that fraction of a second I visualized the thing blowing up as I accomplished my hurdle, but the picture was much too painful to dwell on. I did offer up a quick prayer of thanks when I got to my jeep unscathed.

As soon as I jumped in the jeep the driver gunned it around the corner of the berm and into the highway ditch. I yelled at him to stop so I could scramble up onto the outside of the berm with the radio. He was not happy to have our departure cut short, but I wanted to get a look around and give specific directions to the FAC for the next flight of fighter planes. He'd been waiting for me to come back up on the radio and had fighters stacked up waiting for targets. We began to put in air strikes on the north and east sides of the position. I adjusted the strikes in closer until the FAC requested approval to hit targets he described as danger close. I wasn't sure what danger close meant to him, but at that point everything seemed dangerous and close as far as I was concerned. At any rate he wouldn't accept my next adjustment until I told him I was the battalion senior advisor and gave him my rank and name, and then he put in the next series of fighters.

The artillery trucks pulled out into the ditch and headed south towing the guns, and the jeeps soon followed with the battalion command group and my fellow advisors. All the vehicles were loaded with wounded and dead who needed to be carried out of the position. When the rifle companies began to trot past I moved the air strikes right in next to the far side of the position and shouted to my driver to get ready to go. He was staring at the back end of the jeep, and that's when I saw the rear tires were flat. They had been shot through and it looked like the ride back to Chon Thanh was going to be a bumpy one.

52 Company had been designated the battalion's rear guard and I glanced back across the position as the last of them came scrambling to join me behind the southern berm. They arrived in a shower of dirt just as fifteen or twenty North Vietnamese soldiers in khaki uniforms appeared on the far side of the position, jumping across the northern berm. They were overanxious and all went down kicking and flailing under a furious blast of gunfire from 52 Company.

As the last of the paratroopers began to move to the rear I told the FAC that all friendly troops were out of the position and I wanted him to put the next load of bombs right on top of it. He confirmed that he could see the whole location clearly and said he had fighters on station. I grabbed my radio and jumped into the jeep to discover three wounded paratroopers had taken possession of the back seat and were wedged in between the radios. We all ducked as low as we could and went careening down the ditch as the FAC fired smoke rockets into his new target and jets screamed past and bombs exploded behind us.

The driver was extremely upset about being at the tail end of the battalion, a development he considered a white-knuckle exercise best ameliorated by shoving the gas peddle through the floorboards, clenching his teeth, and muttering a variety of curses. The fact that we were bounding down the ditch on flat tires with people bleeding in the back seat helped focus his aggravation, and he didn't get a grip on his composure until we rejoined the battalion and found the command group a mile south of the now-deserted village of Chon Thanh.

From the Frying Pan into the Fire

The several units of the 1st Airborne Brigade closed into a loose perimeter south of Chon Thanh by five o'clock that afternoon. The brigade headquarters had moved up from Lai Khe and was set up inside the newly established cluster. The artillerymen had already unhooked their guns from the trucks and were back in action by the time I arrived in my wildly bouncing jeep. They were firing north, shelling the old defensive positions the three airborne battalions had just abandoned.

I rejoined my battalion commander just as orders began arriving from the brigade headquarters. The 6th Airborne Battalion had been the trailing unit in our brigade column that day and had been ordered to conduct an airmobile assault later that afternoon to secure a group of low hills located several miles southeast of An Loc. Once that high ground, generally referred to as Windy Hill, was secured, the battalion would construct a firebase on the most prominent feature, Hill 169.

The 5th and 8th Airborne Battalions would be airlifted to the firebase the next day; once on the ground they would move overland to join the troops defending An Loc. The brigade command group and a six-gun battery of 105 mm artillery would also be transported to the new firebase after the two infantry battalions had been delivered. We were told all of the friendly artillery in the An Loc perimeter had been destroyed, so the battery of airborne guns would be a very welcome addition to the garrison's defenses.

Shortly after I found Colonel Hieu he said we were going to do a helicopter reconnaissance of the intended landing zone. I grabbed my map and we joined several officers from the other battalions as a South Vietnamese air force helicopter landed on the highway. Once we were aboard, the aircraft quickly climbed several thousand feet above the hot and dry countryside and headed north toward An Loc, flying well to the east of the highway as we approached the low hills identified as the objective.

My map indicated the countryside was relatively flat and the hill formation, although not very high, was the only readily identifiable terrain feature I could locate in the whole area. From several thousand feet it looked like the hilltops were covered in tall grass. I could also see partially wooded draws snaking down the hillsides into rubber plantations that stretched in all directions. We did one pass over the hills and turned back south so the enemy wouldn't read our intentions and prepare a hot reception for the assault going in later that afternoon.

That was my one fleeting opportunity to study An Loc from the air. I couldn't make out anything very specific. The town and its outskirts were laid out in a grid of streets and the whole place looked like it covered less than a square mile. Most of the buildings seemed to be single story and I couldn't pick out a distinct downtown area. The late-afternoon sun provided highlights through a haze of dust hanging over the town, the only indication of the pounding the defenders were taking from North Vietnamese artillery. Our flight was short and uneventful and the helicopter soon delivered us back on the highway close to our units.

The pickup zone for the upcoming air assault was an open area of abandoned farmland on the east side of the highway, close to the brigade perimeter. By the time we returned from our reconnaissance the 6th Airborne Battalion had established security for itself around the pickup zone in preparation for the arrival of the helicopters. The soldiers were loaded down with rucksacks and weapons, and many were also carrying steel cans of ammunition. Other soldiers carried five-gallon cans of water and the medics had their stretchers folded up, ready to go. The troops had been organized into groups of seven or eight so they could quickly climb into arriving helicopters. The other infantry battalions had rearranged themselves into a loose defensive perimeter around the brigade headquarters and the artillery batteries. Those two battalions put out patrols and established ambushes in preparation for a night of waiting until they could be airlifted north the following morning. What had earlier looked like a massive goat rope was getting itself sorted out.

It was late afternoon when the helicopters arrived to begin airlifting the assaulting battalion. The flight leader radioed for landing instructions and a gaggle of about ten helicopters did a straight-in approach from the south, putting down in a cloud of dirt and noise. They were accompanied by several Cobra gunships that circled the area while waiting to escort the lift helicopters north. As soon as the arriving helicopter's skids hit the ground the first load of paratroopers scrambled aboard. The round trip took about thirty minutes, and the helicopters soon returned for another load of soldiers. There had been a small enemy unit waiting near the landing zone, but the first lift of paratroopers made short work of them. The helicopters accomplished a series of trips back and forth, and the battalion move was completed well before dark.

Later that evening the brigade senior advisor, Colonel Taylor, told me my American lieutenant, Winston Cover, was being reassigned to the 8th Airborne Battalion, which left me with a team of two. That night I rolled up in my nylon poncho liner and got a good night's sleep lying beside the new tires the driver had scrounged for the jeep. Although our artillery continued firing sporadically throughout the night, there was not much activity until early the next morning. The North Vietnamese refocused on us with the rising sun and by 6:00 on the morning of 15 April I was talking to the FAC and adjusting air strikes onto possible enemy locations. We had gotten our first indication the North Vietnamese had a fix on us when mortar rounds began to impact out in our pickup zone and I wanted to put those mortar crews out of action before the helicopters arrived to airlift the rest of the brigade.

I had climbed onto the hood of my jeep to better view the target areas where the air strikes were going in and hadn't noticed any enemy small-arms fire until a bullet smacked into the radiator and bounced around the engine compartment under my boots. Having the jeep shot caused my driver to leap out from behind his steering wheel with another demonstration of unseemly pique. His arm-waving histrionics were incentive enough for me to join the battalion command group out in the pickup area. The battalion was getting organized to load the helicopters scheduled to arrive soon, and it was time for me to shoulder my rucksack and get ready to go.

I grabbed the paratrooper carrying my tactical radio and hustled out into the field where I found Colonel Hieu lying behind a low mound of dirt. We were able to locate him when we saw the long whip antennas that the battalion radio operators were using. I joined the command group just as a stream of enemy machine-gun bullets began to chew into the top of the dirt pile. Some slugs thudded into the mound and others went zipping past, carrying a spray of dirt with them. It seemed the North Vietnamese were maneuvering closer to our pickup area, and at least one machine-gun crew had us under observation. They had undoubtedly seen the long whip antennas just as I had, and their fire was directed specifically at the command group. As I lay there in the growing heat of the early morning sun with dirt sifting down my collar, I was sure the excited chatter on the Vietnamese radios meant someone was getting a patrol out to deal with that machine-gun crew.

Within a few minutes the fire tapered off, but when the helicopters came into view and began their approach there was an upsurge in shooting. Just as the lead helicopter was preparing to land a rocket-propelled grenade, riding a thin trail of white smoke, came whizzing out of the brush. About ten feet above the ground, it whistled past to explode on the far side of the field. The arriving helicopters flared like a flock of startled geese and did a long loop out across the countryside. There was a bit of shouting back and forth before they finally chose to come back and land. It appeared the pilots had a negative view of the incoming fire on the pickup zone, which included several mortar rounds that exploded in the field as I climbed into a helicopter with Colonel Hieu and our radio operators. We all heaved a big sigh of relief as our aircraft lifted off to begin the short flight north, even though we all realized we were trading one kind of gunfight for another.

12

Rangers in Foxholes

The delivery of the 5th and 8th Airborne Battalions, followed by the brigade command group and artillery battery, went off like clockwork on 15 April.[1] The ride north gave me another good look at the whole area from the open doors of the helicopter. Just as I had observed the previous evening, the hills were grass covered with some brush and timber down in the draws. Cobra gunships and tactical air strikes had just completed attacks at the base of the hills and were hitting other potential enemy locations in the surrounding area as our helicopters landed. The air was heavy with the smells of plowed-up earth, shattered vegetation, and burned cordite. The sudden heat on the open hilltop seemed particularly oppressive after the cooling rush of wind everyone had enjoyed during the helicopter ride. As soon as I was back on the ground the sweat began to run, and my steel helmet and rucksack seemed especially heavy.

Within an hour all the 5th Airborne Battalion's soldiers had been delivered from the pickup zone south of Chon Thanh. As the rifle companies got consolidated they spread out into a tactical formation and pushed through the grass to start moving down the northwestern slope toward the rubber plantation. The command group fell in behind the lead company and we were quickly into the cover of the trees at the base of the hill. The heavily laden troops were happy to move out of the open sun and the battalion seemed to simply flow out of sight into the shelter of the rubber trees with an absolute minimum of fuss.

The paratroopers of the 5th Airborne Battalion were tough, experienced, and totally professional, and I was very impressed by what I saw. Our mission was to move across country and establish a defensive position along an old railroad bed on the outskirts of the town. We were to defend the southeastern approaches to An Loc in coordination with the 8th Airborne Battalion, which was off to our left and following its own assigned route toward its objective near the town.

We planned to move into our proposed defensive position well before dark, leaving plenty of time to get dug in. The march through the rubber trees was conducted at a cautious but steady pace, with occasional stops to ensure the squads out on flank security were keeping up with the main body. Inside the rubber plantation the ground was generally flat with occasional dips and low ridges. The dirt was hard packed and brick red and columns of rubber trees marched off into the shade in all directions. Planted in rows, the trees grew about twenty feet apart. It was possible to stand in one place and look down an avenue between the tree trunks in every direction as they were evenly spaced on the ground. They had been planted in a pattern that resembled the checked cornfields of my youth, but on a much-larger scale. Each tree trunk was smooth and about a foot and a half thick with their lowest limbs approximately fifteen feet above the ground. It was hard to tell how tall they actually grew as the tough green leaves were as big as dinner plates and so thick the sky was lost to sight. Chevron cuts in the tree trunks indicated they had been in production. Although many of the cuts were healed, there was an occasional overflowing latex collecting-cup still attached to a tree. Visibility was sometimes as much as fifty yards, but normally less because of folds in the ground and the filtered light.

Even though there was little or no direct sun on the ground it was stifling hot and the sweat was really running. I'd been carrying a rucksack and wearing a steel helmet for years and they had become an integral part of life. Shifting their weight and letting the sweat drip had become something like routine, although their burden seemed particularly telling in that heat. I noticed that not a single soldier walked out in the open avenues between the rows of trees. The men were well spread out and when they paused it was next to a tree trunk to avoid the direct fire that could come down an avenue without warning. The battalion had covered about half the distance from the hilltop landing zone to the city when our forward movement stopped, and Colonel Hieu was called to the front of the lead company. Every soldier found a comfortable place at the foot of a rubber tree and settled in. I walked forward with the battalion commander and was again struck by the silent, nononsense behavior of those paratroopers.

The company commander met us along a slope of rising ground with the news they had found the remains of a South Vietnamese Ranger company. We moved on up to the crest and there they were, every one bloated and sprawled in his own sickening stench. There were fifty or sixty Rangers, each one swollen up and turning black and leaking into the bottom of his

4. This photo of An Loc was taken by Lieutenant Bill Carruthers, an air force FAC who spent many hours over the city. It shows the southern part of town, the area defended by the South Vietnamese army. Smoke marks an air strike going in, and the arrow traces the route followed by the 5th Airborne Battalion into its initial defensive position.

foxhole. They looked like they had been dead for at least a week. The Ranger Company had been dug in and defending a position that stretched for about a hundred yards along the rise of ground where they had been overrun and killed by a North Vietnamese attack. Personal weapons were still with the bodies, but the enemy had taken the hand grenades, claymore antipersonnel mines, and tactical radios. It appeared the North Vietnamese preferred the quality of those particular items over the equipment issued by their own army. I stood there trying to take it all in, looking at those dead soldiers and the Black Panther insignias painted on the fronts of their steel helmets. It took a couple of minutes for me to realize their personal weapons had been left behind because the enemy did not find them valuable. At that moment there was absolutely no question in my mind; we were up against the first team and we were in for a serious fight.

There can be no sadder place than a battlefield where annihilation has oc-curred. The dead soldier's rucksacks had been pulled open and personal let-ters thrown around. Clothing and equipment was also strewn throughout the position and the place was ripe, crawling with flies. Rucksacks and other gear, stained with the sweat and grime of hard wear, lay on the ground forever discarded. Spent small-arms brass and live ammunition littered the position. It was hard to look at the dead soldier's bloody faces and broken heads, torn and shot full of holes, fly covered and rotting in the heat. The bodies were without a shred of dignity, or even humanity. The afternoon was getting along and it was sweltering under the rubber trees as the battalion began to move on across that deserted battlefield. The paratroopers crossed the slope quickly and with few comments. We left the Rangers in their holes to be shoveled into the ground by someone else at some later time.

I had noticed there weren't any North Vietnamese dead in the Ranger's position, but about a hundred yards farther on we walked through a new graveyard. The enemy had collected and buried their own dead in the open avenues between rows of rubber trees. I didn't pause to count the mounds of fresh dirt, but they stretched away like an infestation of large mole hills and there were a lot of them seeding the area.

I had been left with a nagging sense of disquiet when the brigade had failed to break through the North Vietnamese roadblocks on Highway 13. It did not bode well when we were required to hand off our attack to other units and then over-fly the enemy blocking the highway. And now this dramatic example of the enemy's willingness to pay a big price to destroy a company of Rangers added to my growing sense of unease. I knew we were working our way into a hornet's nest.

13

Trying to Not Get Overrun

The lead rifle company was approaching the battalion's designated defensive position later that afternoon when they surprised and killed a detachment of enemy soldiers already dug in along the railroad embankment. That unexpected delay took some time, but the battalion had organized a perimeter and was working to get below ground as dark began to fall. Every man was fully employed digging trenches and fighting positions or felling rubber trees and building bunkers with overhead protection. It surprised me to see long-handled shovels, two-man saws, and axes appear as if by magic. I hadn't noticed anyone carrying that equipment on the way in, but the troops knew what they were doing and the hand tools were put to immediate use. The whole outfit was entrenched with cleared fields of fire in about an hour.

Our new location was on the southeastern outskirts of the town, an area of occasional shacks and stands of bamboo and rubber trees. The primary focus of the position was facing east, the direction from which we had just arrived, and our immediate mission was to block that approach into An Loc. While the neighborhood behind us was supposedly secure, we were not tied in with other friendly units so we established our own security in some ramshackle buildings to our rear. We also pushed observation and listening posts well out into the rubber plantation to our front. A small enemy patrol stumbled into us the next morning and the battalion took three prisoners. The rifle companies were also patrolling aggressively; no one had forgotten the dead Ranger Company we uncovered on our march in from the landing zone. Several small firefights erupted out in the rubber trees later in the day, but the shooting did not distract soldiers inside the battalion perimeter who continued to improve the position. Everyone sensed the hammer was about to fall.[1]

Initially the 1st Airborne Brigade commander, Colonel Le Quang Luong, chose to remain on the newly constructed firebase, but he and his command group moved into the city on 16 April, the day after our air assault. Taking a security detail from the battalion on the hill, Colonel Luong and Colonel Taylor moved across country without serious incident and took up residence in a large bunker in An Loc. While the brigade commander was getting relocated, the enemy was not idle. The new airborne firebase on Windy Hill was about to undergo a massive and devastating attack, and at the same time the 5th Airborne Battalion and I would undergo our own memorable trial by fire. Later, when there was time to step back from my own experience and consider those two fights as parts of a larger event, it became apparent the enemy had coordinated them carefully. Timed to preclude either of the airborne battalions from helping the other, both of those fights were serious efforts to destroy a major part of the 1st Airborne Brigade.

The hilltop firebase had begun to take an increasing volume of enemy fire on the seventeenth, and because it was on the only high ground in the vicinity, and equally prominent on maps, it was easy to see and target. Much of the initial incoming fire was from North Vietnamese mortars ranging in on the paratrooper's positions. Then enemy artillery, located well to the north of An Loc, also began to search for the firebase. The volume of artillery fire gradually increased and the accuracy improved, indicating rounds were being adjusted by enemy forward observers. At the same time the North Vietnamese conducted a series of ground probes that tested and mapped the hilltop defenses. Those events were all good indicators that the firebase was about to be subjected to serious attention. Pressure intensified throughout the eighteenth and nineteenth. We learned later that two North Vietnamese infantry regiments with six tanks in support had been given the mission of destroying the firebase.

The defending paratroopers certainly had no shortage of targets. They directed tactical air strikes flown by carrier-based navy and Marine Corps jets as well as air force fighter planes against the attacking North Vietnamese. U.S. Army Cobra gunships flying nonstop also engaged the enemy with minigun and rocket fire. The volume of air support increased as the enemy's attacks intensified and U.S. Air Force Spectre AC-130 gunships were on station and working for the defenders throughout the night. At least one B-52 strike was accomplished in direct support of the firebase, and by the twentieth several of the artillery pieces on the hill had been destroyed by enemy fire and the rest were blasting point-blank into the enemy who were threatening to breach the defensive wire. The paratroopers could also hear armored vehicles coming up the northern slopes.

The 6th Airborne Battalion's senior advisor, Lieutenant Ross Kelly, who had replaced Major Richard Morgan when he was wounded and medevaced, provided an ongoing description while coordinating defensive fires for the paratroopers. At the same time I was fully employed with my own battle in the southeastern outskirts of the town, which I will describe next. But even while I was feeling hard pressed, the enemy had successfully invested and was massing against the hilltop firebase. The paratroopers had begun to take serious casualties as the battle unfolded; the enemy suffered terrible losses to include the destruction of all six of their tanks. But the North Vietnamese poured more troops into the assault, and when it became clear they were going to overrun the position the hard-pressed defenders were ordered to break out before they were overwhelmed. The paratroopers ensured that all six of their artillery pieces has been destroyed before fighting their way off the hill.[2]

Hours later the 6th Airborne Battalion commander, Lieutenant Colonel Nguyen Van Dinh, came back up on the air. He and Lieutenant Kelly had organized the surviving paratroopers and were on the move. There was no chance for them to join the An Loc defenses. In fact they were being forced to the southeast, farther away from the city, by an enemy intent on killing or capturing them to the last man.

After a running fight that further whittled down their numbers, some of the exhausted survivors were picked up by helicopters and others succeeded in walking out and eventually linking up with friendly units. Colonel Dinh immediately began the process of reconstituting his battalion. As a footnote to that event and as an example of how the Vietnamese Airborne Division operated in combat, Colonel Dinh's battalion was quickly brought back up to strength. The new 6th Airborne Battalion was built around the survivors from the firebase fight and included about two hundred men transferred from the military prison in Saigon. The battalion was back in action along Highway 13 in less than a month and was the first unit to eventually reach the southern outskirts of An Loc.

While the enemy was initially getting ready to overrun the firebase, the 5th Airborne Battalion hadn't attracted much enemy fire. We had continued to busy ourselves preparing our position, but as the attack on the firebase developed we also began to feel North Vietnamese pressure. When the enemy chased in our observation posts on 18 April we knew we would not be ignored much longer. Firefights erupted along the east side of the perimeter during the next twenty-four hours and it looked like the North Vietnamese were getting positioned to kick off a major attack on our position, even as they were overwhelming the firebase. A late-afternoon barrage of incoming mortar rounds on the nineteenth told us to get ready, and when the enemy came charging through the rubber trees they were cut down by the dozens.

It was a full-blown assault with green tracers and rocket–propelled grenades flying through the trees, smacking into logs and dirt. I was reminded of other gunfights in other obscure places during previous tours. The action was hot and heavy while it lasted, but as darkness began to fall the attack fizzled in bursts of friendly small-arms fire emphasized by several air strikes.

The enemy reinforced during the night and early on the twentieth their next attack started with mortar and small-arms fire that rapidly increased in volume. Our red tracers zipped out into the rubber plantation while sheets of incoming green tracers scythed through the trees and brush in a steadily increasing volume. The growing roar of small-arms fire was punctuated by the crunch and bang of rocket-propelled grenades and mortar rounds hitting trees and throwing up clouds of dirt. A haze of smoke and dust cut visibility and the stink of explosives thickened as the battle developed. The attack was fast becoming a bigger fight than anything I'd seen for a long time as incoming fire continued to build and the paratrooper's defensive fires became deafening. An air force FAC was overhead cycling in flight after flight of tactical aircraft that I directed onto the enemy. I also put air strikes onto the most likely staging areas the enemy might be using, and through it all the pressure only seemed to intensify.

Our wounded were being treated in the fighting positions because of the heavy volume of incoming fire. The battalion's medics were waiting for a lull in the attack to move the wounded to the rear, but there was no lull. In the early afternoon the battalion's forward positions reported hearing engine noise to their front. While it was difficult to tell the exact direction and distance to the enemy vehicles, I studied my map and put air strikes onto what I considered their most likely locations. Enemy soldiers pushed forward regardless of the defensive fires we were generating, and it was becoming apparent we were about to be smothered by the North Vietnamese avalanche. I'd never been involved in that kind of situation before, a battalion being overrun and destroyed by waves of attacking infantry. It was a sobering experience.

Sheets of green tracers were skipping across the ground and tearing at the trees. Dozens of rocket-propelled grenades came flying through the position, some high in the branches and others low enough to hit bunkers, throwing blasts of sparks and shrapnel as they detonated. Mortar rounds slammed into tree limbs and blasted clouds of dirt as they impacted in and all around the perimeter. The North Vietnamese seemed to have an inexhaustible supply of mortar ammunition, and their troops attacked right through the impact area on their way into our position. The whole battalion was becoming engulfed in an all-consuming battle for survival, and I recognized that if we didn't do something different our options were rapidly being narrowed to a single outcome—we were about to go down fighting. Colonel Hieu had been providing periodic updates to Colonel Luong, the brigade commander. They must have arrived at the same conclusion because the battalion was ordered to disengage and move to a new defensive position on the south side of town. We got the order just as enemy infantry were being killed in our forward trenches.

The battalion was going to move less than a mile, first through a rubber plantation and then around a burned-over area covered with scrub brush. Colonel Hieu ordered the 51 Company commander to defend the forward edge of the battalion's position. The stay-behind company was to provide cover for the rest of the battalion as it pulled back and moved to the new location. Several flights of fighter planes were on station and I told Colonel Hieu that Sergeant McCauley would go with him; I wanted to put in those air strikes and intended to stay until that job was complete. Colonel Hieu's answer was immediate and made the situation crystal clear. After quickly pointing out the direction the battalion was going to move, he grabbed me by the shirt and pulled me close. Looking me directly in the eye and shouting over the roar of gunfire, he gave me a message I will never forget—Do not stay here long: 51 Company will die today.

I'd previously studied the theory of the Detachment-Left-In-Contact in service schools. Although I had not thought through all the human implications, I understood the concept of how a larger unit can break contact with the enemy by ordering one of its subordinate units to fight for time. 51 Company was going to stay in place and make that fight. Their mission was to force the enemy to concentrate on them while the rest of the battalion moved. The company would soon be locked in a deadly embrace it would not be able to break. It was going to make a stand so the rest of the battalion could fight the next battle. In a couple of minutes I saw groups of soldiers, loaded with gear, running back through the trees and the command group fell in with one of the rifle companies as it moved past. Then they were gone.

On one level I understood what was going on, but things were happening fast and the harsh realities had not fully sunk in. I knew I didn't want to be unexpectedly trapped in a bunker, so I spent the next ten minutes lying in a depression behind a rubber tree, shouting instructions to the FAC. Extremely heavy automatic fire was flying through the position, tearing off bark and creating a blizzard of falling leaves. The noise level had reached an ear-shattering crescendo. Layers of smoke and dust were drifting across the ground, cutting visibility. The soldier carrying my radio was laying to my right, within arm's reach. He had the radio in his backpack and the spaghetti cord connecting it to the handset was stretched out between us.

I have a very clear mental picture of several paratroopers moving back from the forward positions. For a second I thought they were drifting to the rear, looking for a way out, but then my eye caught a flash of color—their headgear. They had thrown away their helmets and pulled on their maroon paratrooper berets, and they were backing into recently vacated foxholes. Committed to a fight they could not possibly win, those men understood the ramifications of their orders and had decided to face their enemies wearing the symbol that best described who they were. I realized with a jolt they were actually getting ready to die right then and there, in that patch of torn-up rubber plantation.

Seeing their willingness to accept their fate, their own impending deaths, really shocked me. I was looking at something on a level totally different from a firefight where men expect to win and walk away. An outcome was unfolding right in front of me, beyond anything I had ever before experienced, and it was coming together fast. I saw what they were doing, I understood it, I could not get my head around the finality of it. I also had no intention of joining them in their Vietnamese Valhalla, but the reality of how those soldiers embraced their impossible mission was stunning. It has forever colored my view of how I should respond to the lesser, the nonfatal crises that life occasionally presents.

The next flight of fighters was loaded with hard bombs and napalm and I directed the FAC to put it right in front of the trench line. There was a momentary pause in the enemy's volume of fire with the blast and heat of the bombs exploding and the napalm searing through the rubber trees immediately to our front. If I was going to move I had to do it right then. I yelled at the soldier carrying my radio and jumped up to go. He was lying on his belly with his helmet hiding his face. When he didn't respond I grabbed him by a shoulder. His body was slack and loose, and then I realized he was dead. I hadn't heard him make a sound when he got hit. He was lying within arm's reach and had been shot through the head and I hadn't even noticed. I jerked the radio out of his backpack and started to run.

The noise of the fight began to pick up again as I ran bent over, loaded with gear and carrying my shotgun in one hand and the radio in the other. Green tracers were cutting through the trees all around as leaves and bark rained down. The humid heat was taking its toll; I was soaked with sweat. I'd covered about fifty yards when I heard the FAC on the radio. He was telling me the next flight of fighters was on station and ready to put in their ordnance. I fell into a dip in the ground and tried to catch my breath as I listened to the noise of the battle I'd just left. There was still a lot of shooting so I told him to put the air strike on the friendly side of where the napalm had gone in. As the fast movers came screaming over I jumped up and ran again. In another fifty yards I was ready to take another breather.

As I lay gasping and sweating on the ground, the volume of fire behind me began to taper off. The enemy was overrunning the position, and while there were occasional bursts of shooting it appeared the fight was all but over. The FAC had several more flights ready to go and I told him to put them directly on the position. He wanted to know if that was where I was still located and I answered that I'd moved and the stay-behind unit had been overrun. That was the right target because I knew the enemy was concentrating there. After a pause he repeated his question. I told him again that he had the correct target and I wanted him to put everything available on the battalion's old defensive position. The air strikes came in one after another as I trudged out of the shelter of the rubber plantation and into the direct sun that was baking the burned-over area. The ground was covered with wiry grass and tough, charred knee-high brush, and every step kicked up clouds of soot.

I was intent on catching up with the battalion, so instead of skirting the long way around I took a calculated risk and cut straight across the open area. I began to run out of gas about halfway across, so I found another dip in the ground to fall into. As I lay there, leaning back and sweating on my ruck-sack, I could see the FAC's aircraft circling high overhead. I listened on his frequency as he continued to put air strikes into the old battalion position, and then I suddenly saw a string of smoke puffs appear across the sky behind his little airplane. After a pause I heard the pop, pop, pop of shells exploding in the clear blue sky. The FAC was being shot at by antiaircraft artillery, the shells exploding not far behind him, just like a World War II movie and I seemed to be the only person in the theater.

I broke into the FAC's transmissions and told him what I was seeing. He acknowledged and began to climb and circle away as the last of the air strikes went screaming by. The enemy had arrived on the An Loc battlefield with 37 mm antiaircraft cannon and the even more lethal radar-controlled ZSU-57s mounted on tank chassis. I was watching some of that firepower in action, although the exploding antiaircraft shells seemed remote from my little piece of dirt. While I could hear the shells popping as the smoke puffs walked across the sky far above, I couldn't hear the antiaircraft guns that were firing at the elusive FAC.

Once the show was over I struggled back to my feet and continued across the last of the open area and found the battalion. I was drained and my uniform was sweat soaked and filthy. The troops had moved into another plantation of rubber trees and were already digging in when I arrived. The new position was a half mile south of An Loc, on the east side of Highway 13.

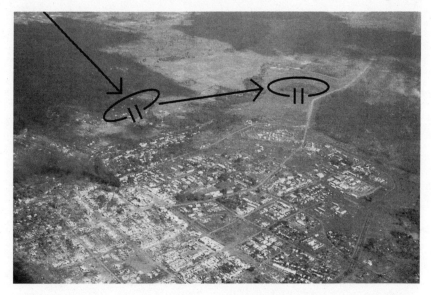

5. The arrow traces the movement of the 5th Airborne Battalion from its initial defensive position to the second position it occupied on the south side of An Loc. Photo courtesy of Lieutenant Bill Carruthers.

I found the battalion commander and dumped my gear on the ground. He saw I was there, but was busy and didn't question me. As I looked around I noticed soldiers carrying loaded stretchers struggling through the position. Four men were gripping the corner handles of each load, and two or three dead paratroopers had been tied onto each stretcher. Their slack arms and legs were swinging with the movement as the carrying parties arrived. Those dead soldiers had been killed in the old position and were being carried in by their buddies. They were buried later that day on the north side of our new perimeter, at the edge of the trees between us and the town. Other soldiers were carrying the extra weapons and gear and helping the wounded as they struggled to get situated.

While soldiers had reported hearing tanks earlier in the day I hadn't seen any and didn't know if the air strikes I put in killed any of them. If not, it wasn't for a lack of trying. The battle for the hilltop firebase, which occurred roughly during the same time span, attracted a lot of attention, and rightly so as the loss of an infantry battalion plus the newly arrived artillery battery was a serious blow. The larger message to the South Vietnamese was that the enemy could take on two paratrooper battalions simultaneously, with equally serious intent and almost equally catastrophic results.

Over the next several days a handful of 51 Company soldiers rejoined the battalion. They had somehow survived the fight in the old position and managed to link up with friendly troops in An Loc. From there they had been able to locate us. But all the 51 Company officers and sergeants were gone, and the few surviving soldiers who filtered in were assigned to other companies. Just as Colonel Hieu had told me, 51 Company had been ordered to stand and fight, and now it was dead.

14
New Digs

The 5th Airborne Battalion's new defensive perimeter was quickly laid out and the soldiers started to dig in. The long-handled shovels, saws, and axes reappeared and were put to immediate use. Bunkers and fighting positions began to take shape while rubber trees were dropped and their trunks cut into lengths for overhead cover. We had been in the new position several hours when three artillery shells suddenly came screaming in from the north. They were a rude introduction to our new home and provided a first clue to what the An Loc garrison had been experiencing. The attention-getting arrival of those first shells, accompanied by serious explosions out in the rubber trees, caused the soldiers to get serious and dirt began to fly in earnest. While no one was injured by those first three rounds, every man knew that more would undoubtedly follow. We just didn't have any idea of the intensity and duration of the torment that was about to unfold.

During the next several days more big artillery shells whistled into our patch of rubber trees. They all arrived out of the north and it appeared they were probably intended for An Loc, but because we were on the gun-target line we were getting a few overflying rounds. Very soon, however, artillery began to impact closer to our perimeter, and more often. Then several came screaming right in with us. If the initial rounds were a coincidence because we'd moved into an unfortunate location, we soon began to suspect that North Vietnamese artillery crews had learned where we were and were shifting some of their attention to us in a more specific and personal way.

The battalion ran patrols out into the rubber plantation starting the first afternoon and the enemy was soon located forward of our perimeter. Some of the North Vietnamese followed our patrols back in, and once the enemy figured out where the battalion was located they began a process of adjusting their mortars to target us. Everyone in the battalion quickly became adept at responding to incoming artillery and mortar rounds. The men kept an ear cocked and disappeared from sight with magical speed at the first hint of danger. Once individual fighting positions and the command group's bunker had been completed, a trench was dug to connect the perimeter. The soldiers also worked hard installing barbed-wire entanglements forward of the perimeter as soon as carrying parties were able to bring rolls of wire out from the town.

Our position was within a hundred yards of Highway 13 and we quickly established a good link with our sister unit, the 8th Airborne Battalion, directly across the road to the west. The primary focus of our defense faced into the rubber plantation to the south and southeast, although soldiers were dug in all around the perimeter. It was approximately a hundred yards across the position and grazing fire covered every approach. The command bunker was located near the center. Six feet deep and ten feet square, it was covered with several layers of rubber tree trunks and piled high with dirt. The battalion commander, the operations officer, and several radio operators made it their home and seldom emerged. Our battalion surgeon established a small underground aid station nearby.

While I initially spent a lot of time in the command bunker, I also had an individual position dug for myself. It was constructed by digging a trench three feet wide, ten feet long, and four feet deep. The trench was then covered with a layer of rubber tree logs and a heaping pile of dirt, leaving an uncovered opening at one end for access. The overhead cover might have taken a hit from a mortar round, but it would have been fatal to be at home if a heavier artillery shell were to knock on my door. When not in the command bunker I was in residence in my personal little refuge. As the battalion position solidified and the pace of operations became focused on our defense, I was able to coordinate supporting fires from my private office, my hole in the ground. A routine developed that included cringing from the shelling, sleeping, or sitting on my rucksack at the open end of my modest abode so I could peer out while talking on my tactical radio. I had decided to continue carrying it after my radio operator had been killed. It was simply more convenient for me to keep the radio in my rucksack and get replacement batteries from the battalion's radio operators when required. Besides, considering the growing number of casualties the battalion was suffering, I didn't want to take a soldier away from the perimeter.

When business was slack and I was able to sleep I crawled to the far end of my covered trench, pulled off my boots, and wrapped up in my nylon poncho liner to escape the mosquitoes. I piled my helmet, rucksack, shotgun, and radio between me and the open end to take the blast if a mortar round should try to seek me out. The raw dirt and latex-leaking logs provided a certain garden fragrance as well as a rustic ambiance that appeared to grow on me with time. I never suffered from claustrophobia even though it was a bit confining and perpetually dark and dank. The Vietnamese probably thought me a bit strange, spending time by myself and not living on top of others as they preferred. My little hidey-hole provided a safe refuge from small-arms fire and shrapnel, but when artillery shells came blasting into the area all semblance of false security evaporated. There was no way to escape tensed muscles, a parched mouth, and a gut-wrenching sense of vulnerability with artillery rounds impacting close by. It was a very serious game of chance. Then I would lay sweating with an arm across my face, trying to keep the sifting dirt out of my eyes while rewording and perfecting various promises to the Almighty.

I spent many hours, both during the day and in the dark of interminable nights, sitting on my rucksack with my head sticking out of my little bunker. My radio antenna stood there beside me as I communicated with an overhead FAC, the crew of a Cobra helicopter, or one of the big American air force gunships. Keeping the brigade advisor in An Loc current on the battalion's situation was also important, but I knew he was monitoring my radio frequency so talking to him directly was not routine. That radio was my only link to the fire support so essential to the battalion. It was also my only connection to other American voices as I had become a one-man act. Sergeant McCauley, the other half of my already diminished team, was moved to our sister battalion across the road to replace an advisor who had been wounded and evacuated.

My bunker was close to an enormous bomb crater that had been blown in the ground during some previous battle. The crater was about fifteen feet across and perhaps ten feet deep, with a puddle of muddy water at the bottom. The sides of the crater were steep, and the soil was soft and greasy. The surrounding rubber trees had either been blown away or stripped of their leaves when that big bomb had gone off, so I could see a piece of sky in that direction.

Several mornings after we moved into the position I noticed a soldier about halfway down into the crater. He hadn't been there the evening before, but sometime during the night he'd gotten into the crater and was clinging to the slope. He didn't appear to be wounded, but he didn't have a weapon and had lost his gear and helmet. Filthy and wild-eyed, he was conscious but totally unresponsive when I tried to get his attention. As the day progressed he slid deeper into the crater and eventually came to rest in the water at the bottom. I pointed him out to several soldiers, expecting the medics or possibly his buddies would pull him out and care for him.

The following morning he was still there, semiconscious and totally covered with mud and cowering in the water at the bottom of the crater. It was obvious none of the soldiers in the area had any intention of helping him. Later that morning I checked in with Colonel Hieu in the command bunker, and during our conversation I mentioned the plight of the soldier in the crater. The battalion commander seemed to know about him, but wasn't interested in discussing him. I persisted, saying that the soldier needed to be pulled out and cared for, but the response I got was not positive.

I fully appreciated that many Vietnamese are embarrassed by physical and mental disabilities, and Colonel Hieu was simply not willing to discuss a soldier he viewed as an embarrassment to the battalion as well as to himself. I did not go to the battalion surgeon directly, sensitive to potential chain-of-command issues with the battalion commander. Much to my relief the soldier had disappeared from the crater by the following morning. He was one of the few airborne soldiers I observed suffering a serious mental breakdown. Considering the conditions under which we were fighting it was a wonder there weren't more.

The mortar rounds impacting in and around the battalion's position became persistent, and they were deadly. At times that incoming fire seemed to grow to a crescendo that felt almost overwhelming. They were 82 mm weapons fired by the North Vietnamese units pushing against us from the rubber plantation. Because the enemy had traced our perimeter and knew exactly where we were, their mortar attacks became extremely accurate compared to the incoming artillery that seemed to arrive by chance. But under either circumstance there was no escaping the fear when the ground began to shudder. I tried every possible distraction, rehiking a rocky crest in the Black Hills, reswimming SCUBA dives over coral reefs, reliving the passionate embrace of an enthusiastic redheaded girl in Chicago, but nothing could overcome the realities of the moment when explosions filled the world. Alone in the dark, dirt in my mouth, screaming shells coming into the position and taking apart the landscape, I was scared stiff. The only consolation was knowing that if an artillery round hit my refuge directly or a mortar round joined me through the uncovered entrance it would all be over in a flash.

Although there were periods of relative quiet, the enemy was right up against our perimeter and every day saw some kind of incoming fire, either indirect mortars and artillery or direct small arms, or both. On a number of occasions attacks were fierce, as I was recently reminded when reading a copy of the daily log kept by advisors in the province headquarters bunker in An Loc. The following entry was made on Wednesday, 26 April 1972: "5th and 8th Airborne Battalions under attack from 0500 hours until 1700 hours, preceded by one of the heaviest mortar barrages concentrated in one area—over 600 rounds." The next log entry for that day notes three enemy tanks in the northeastern outskirts and seven others on the northwestern side of town. An entry for Sunday, 30 April 1972, states, "2030 hours heavy contact with 5th and 8th Airborne Battalions—mortar barrage lasted 20 minutes. Spectre [a U.S. Air Force AC-130 gunship that was ever present after dark] and FAC were sent."

Artillery fire continued to arrive from the north and dozens of rounds of various sizes came right into the position. In addition to the Chinese- and Soviet-supplied artillery the enemy brought from Cambodia, they also turned a number of American guns on us that the South Vietnamese had abandoned during the early days of the offensive. That captured artillery included both 105 mm and 155 mm weapons, and all were integrated into the North Vietnamese forces very effectively. A large stockpile of ammunition had also been lost early on, and it was being shot at the An Loc defenders. The results became mind numbing as a seemingly endless stream of shells tore down trees and smothered the position in dirt and rubbish.

The enemy had an organized and effective logistics system supported by convoys of trucks that worked hard to keep their forward troops supplied and their guns firing. There were times, however, when the intensity of the enemy's ground and artillery attacks tapered off and we were able to get out of our bunkers to peer around at the new devastation. Soldiers used those lulls to shovel out the forward trench line and repair the defensive wire as much as possible. It was clear to everyone, however, that the overall intensity of the battle was increasing as the days went by. Much of the plantation near the battalion's position had been uprooted or smashed. The trees and stumps still standing were peppered and slashed by shrapnel. Tree limbs and trash covered the ground and the rubber trees bled streams of white latex into the red dirt.

Water parties periodically made a dangerous journey to a jungle stream a quarter of a mile east of our position. The water was stagnant and I laced my replenished canteens with iodine purification tablets. After years of drinking that stuff it seemed I'd actually acquired a taste for it. While there was usually enough drinking water, I was seldom able to wash my face and I shaved even less frequently. My uniform was so impregnated with sweat and the local red dirt that the camouflage pattern had become hard to see. I had never been that filthy before in my life. The accretion of grubbiness was gradual and my senses seemed to make the necessary adjustments as my hygienic condition worsened. Since there was no way to get cleaned up I had no choice but to embrace my trampish situation. The fighting positions and bunkers also served as bathrooms as no one was willing to respond to nature's call out in the open. The troops and I cleaned out our abodes with improvised shovels, throwing dirt and filth out of our holes like so many prairie dogs.

The demands of fighting that part of the An Loc battle were persistent and unrelenting. Firefights on the battalion's perimeter flared up at all hours of the day and night, and I was fully absorbed in coordinating defensive fires. I also kept busy directing air strikes against enemy assembly areas or nearby mortar positions in an effort to disrupt their attacks. When I heard the thump of a mortar firing I would quickly get an approximate azimuth and distance to get a fix on the weapon and then go after it using the airpower available, either Cobra gunships or fast moving tactical fighters. The enemy knew exactly where we were, and they also knew we intended to continue defending the southern approaches to An Loc, so they zeroed in on us and concentrated their efforts.

North Vietnamese ground attacks were accompanied by volumes of automatic fire marked by a storm of green tracers crisscrossing the position, and it was important to never forget there were several unmarked rounds between every tracer. A stream of machine-gun bullets chopping through the brush demanded unblinking attention, and I made every effort to stay out of their way. Enemy infantry attacks were usually accompanied by dozens of rocket-propelled grenades smacking trees and throwing fiery blasts of shrapnel as mortar rounds exploded in and around the position. The noise was much more than one might expect—at times shattering, overwhelming.

Through it all, day and night, enemy artillery continued to whistle in from the north. Whether our position was their intended target or not made little difference as the impact on us was the same. Some of the big shells sighed and some screamed, and some arrived totally unannounced to surprise, blast, tear, and kill. The paratroopers of the 5th Airborne Battalion dug their holes deeper, shot every living thing that tried to get close to their positions, and refused to allow the enemy into An Loc from the south.

15
Airborne Rangers into the Breach

The South Vietnamese army's strategic reconnaissance unit was the 81st Airborne Ranger Group, a battalion-sized outfit. It was organized around teams of highly motivated and very experienced soldiers whose primary mission was to conduct long-range patrols and combat raids into the most inaccessible corners of the country. They also did cross-border operations. Trained and equipped for those types of special operations missions, their advisors were highly trained American Special Forces officers and senior sergeants who volunteered to serve with them. I knew the South Vietnamese army was running out of resources when the Airborne Rangers were thrown into the battle to fight as a conventional infantry unit.

Burning up the army's most valuable strategic reconnaissance unit in a ground combat role had to be a last option. But at that point the outcome of the battle was very much in doubt and no other unit was available that possessed the experience, ability, and absolute fidelity to the mission that marked the Airborne Rangers, and that made them expendable.

We were alerted they would be moving through our area soon after we began establishing our new position next to Highway 13. They had also done an airmobile insertion southeast of the city, similar to the one that had introduced us to the fight. While they knew where we were located, we had to be particularly alert to their approach because of their unconventional appearance. Although the Airborne Rangers were not part of the Vietnamese Airborne Division, the men of both organizations were cut from the same bolt of material. Battalion officers and sergeants knew men in the Airborne Rangers as many had trained or served together on previous assignments. There were heart-felt greetings and warm handshakes as they moved past our perimeter on their way to engage the enemy in the city. Colonel Hieu made a point of greeting the Airborne Ranger commander, Major Pham Van

Voeng. Saris bi thương ở đồi Đồng Long, An Lộc 1972

6. An Airborne Ranger comforts a wounded buddy during the battle. Photo courtesy of the 81st Airborne Ranger Group & Vietnamese Special Forces Association.

Huan, who was a tough-looking hombre. I later learned two American advisors were with the unit, but I didn't pick them out of that shaggy-haired crew slipping through the rubber trees.

The Airborne Rangers certainly were a motley-looking bunch. Some of them had just been extracted from a cross-border mission in the Cambodian jungles with no opportunity to catch their breath. The whole outfit was a weapon in the fully cocked position. They were armed with everything under the sun to include weapons taken from the enemy. Their uniforms were equally diverse with some soldiers in camouflage and others in mixed uniforms. Some of them were wearing steel helmets and others had on soft caps. If there was one common feature they all shared to a remarkable degree, it was that they were the toughest-looking crew I had seen in many a moon. That was saying a lot because up until that point the paratroopers I was serving with were as ferocious as any soldiers I had ever laid eyes on.

Within hours of moving into An Loc the Airborne Rangers launched a night attack to clear the enemy from an area that threatened the integrity of the garrison's defense. While not organized or equipped as conventional infantry, they certainly knew how to fight with enthusiasm. The Airborne Rangers possessed extraordinary bravery and were supremely confident, and they took terrific casualties while destroying the enemy in their objective area. The survivors were then ordered to dig in and defend a key portion of the garrison's perimeter, and over the next several weeks they defeated a series of persistent North Vietnamese attacks in their sector. When the unit was eventually withdrawn from An Loc, it reported sixty-one men killed and approximately three hundred wounded.[1]

The Airborne Rangers accomplished their mission, but during that furious combat the finest strategic reconnaissance unit in the Vietnamese army was irrevocably crippled. It had taken years to develop that outfit's specialized capabilities and much was lost when they were used up in the battle for An Loc.

16

Tactical Arc Lights

Arc Light was the code name for the massive attacks carried out by B-52D Stratofortress bombers throughout the course of the Vietnam War. During the first three years I served in Vietnam I heard the thunder of Arc Light attacks being delivered many times, but they were always in the distance because the big bombers normally targeted enemy locations far from friendly troops. As an infantry officer I had viewed the B-52 as a strategic rather than a tactical weapon since their attacks did not directly affect the immediate ground battles in which I'd been involved.

Arc Light missions normally consisted of several groups of aircraft, called cells, of three B-52s each. They flew so high they were often out of sight and sound of their targets far below. The three aircraft in each cell flew in echelon, and as they approached their release point they positioned themselves to ensure their bombs would saturate the target area. An Arc Light strike resulted in complete devastation as each aircraft was loaded with eighty-four 500-pound bombs carried internally and twenty-four 750-pound bombs on hard points under the wings. If two cells totaling six bombers were hitting a target, a fairly common occurrence, they combined to deliver a grand total of 360,000 pounds of high-explosive destruction into a very restricted space in a period of only a few minutes.[1]

The geographic area an Arc Light attack went into was called a box, and each box was designed for a specific type of target. The targets in the vicinity of An Loc were primarily enemy troop concentrations, and the footprints of the boxes were roughly a half mile long and a quarter mile wide. Bomb craters often overlapped throughout a target box; no one wanted to be very close to the business end of an Arc Light attack.

During the years before I joined Team 162 I had seen the breathtaking results of Arc Light missions on several occasions. The high explosives delivered by a B-52 strike created a shattered and dust-riddled disaster. Every living thing was shocked senseless or killed, giant trees were shredded and torn apart, and pulverized rock covered the whole area with a gray powder that only emphasized the terrible destruction. Once-lush jungle was blasted into a giant tangle of splintered junk almost impossible to climb through, and the surviving trickle of water in fractured streambeds was filthy and seemed to puddle aimlessly. During the battle for An Loc the air force shifted B-52s from attacking strategic targets in distant places to supporting the An Loc garrison in a very direct and immediate way. While B-52s had bombed in close proximity to the defenders of Khe Sanh several years before, the tactical Arc Light was reborn at An Loc when target boxes were drawn all around the outskirts of the town and loads of bombs began to fall close to friendly troops.

What once had been the sound of distant thunder now became a compelling and growing hurricane of explosion that was delivered with dramatic effect. As the battle for An Loc progressed, Arc Light attacks took place at all hours of the day and night, and many were in the immediate vicinity of the town. When an attack was going to go in nearby I wanted to be to the side of the target box rather than on either the approach or the exit end. I was fairly confident the aircraft would be lined up properly to go down the length of the box, but I did worry about getting caught in an early or late release of bombs. Since I was not involved in drawing target boxes, I never knew exactly where they were located or the approach direction of the aircraft. So when the bombs began to fall I just tried to crawl inside my helmet while making repetitious and fevered protestations to the Almighty. Even one errant bomb hitting the battalion's position would certainly have been one too many.

Normally we had a heads-up when an Arc Light was on the way, but in some cases they just suddenly arrived with a thundering roar that shook the whole world and caused clouds of pulverized rubber trees and dirt to drift in the wind. Every tactical Arc Light was potentially very dangerous to the defending troops, and it was a real compliment to the crews in those B-52s that every strike was delivered in its intended box. Week after week the bombers blasted concentrations of enemy units either forming up to attack or in some cases actually in the process of closing in on the city's defensive perimeter. Perhaps the most-intense example of targeting occurred during the major North Vietnamese attacks starting on 11 May when the first cell of B-52s unloaded their bombs at 5:30 A.M. That mission was followed by a series of missions that arrived at fifty-five-minute intervals for the rest of the day.

As the battle developed, B-52 missions became almost routine, if such an event can ever be described in such prosaic terms. While familiarity may breed contempt on a personal level, that type of outcome is definitely not the case with an Arc Light. During the month of April, as an example, 363 attacks were delivered against the North Vietnamese, and almost all of them were targeted against enemy units in the immediate vicinity of An Loc or along Highway 13. While the Arc Lights that impacted within a mile or so of my location tended to blend into the background noise of the larger battle, some attacks were much closer and they made the earth move. In several noteworthy instances the closest side of a target box had been drawn within a quarter mile of my little bunker. That might not seem particularly significant considering that over the years I had put in a lot of air strikes much closer than that which included big bombs. While it is true that my pain threshold had become elevated, I soon learned the cumulative effect of repeated B-52 attacks is something very different from any other kind of air strike.

When we were notified that an Arc Light was going to be close, we took advantage of all the protection available. There was no preliminary noise of falling bombs or any other indication when it happened. I don't know where Hollywood got the idea of whistling bombs, but it wasn't from B-52 strikes. Everyone anticipated the event by curling up in the fetal position with their helmets pulled down tight and their teeth and all their muscles clinched. As the first load of bombs started to walk across the earth, trees and buildings began to quake and a growing crescendo of noise filled the air. In some cases trees and buildings simply fell down with an additional crash. No matter how tightly one pressed into the ground or up against a wall, the trembling and jerking and rolling of a nearby B-52 attack was dramatic and unsettling.

Once the bombs began to hit, the blast and concussion didn't let up and it seemed to intensify as each succeeding load of bombs arrived. When it was finally over, everyone stayed frozen in place for a couple of minutes just to be sure, then people would begin to look around, blinking and rubbing the dirt out of their eyes. The troops often seemed a bit dazed, but also thankful that none of the bombs had come out the near side of the box. We were also very grateful that we could call on such enormous destruction and direct it against our enemies with such gratifying results.

I recall two instances when we knew Arc Light strikes had been particularly effective. One of the battalion's radio operators spent a lot of time searching frequencies in an effort to locate the enemy's transmissions. When he successfully found the enemy talking, he and Colonel Hieu would huddle together and listen in. Normally the North Vietnamese practiced good communications security, but on occasion we could match up what we heard with an enemy unit and sometimes even figure out a location on the ground. In one case we heard a North Vietnamese regimental commander order his

7. B-52D Stratofortress bomber of the type that delivered over 700 Arc Light attacks in the vicinity of An Loc during April and May 1972. Photo courtesy of the U.S. Air Force.

battalions to move into the fresh bomb craters created by a B-52 strike just delivered. I'm sure he thought that lightning wouldn't strike the same place twice, so his troops could safely hunker down in a still-smoking Arc Light box. He hadn't counted on the flexibility of the U.S. Air Force, who quickly responded to the information we were able to provide through my encrypted radio link. The North Vietnamese troops had been in their new bomb craters about an hour when an in-flight B-52 mission was retargeted to hit them. The strike arrived with no warning and the enemy regiment was simply destroyed. At least there was only silence when our radio operator asked them how they liked their rude surprise.

In the second case we were listening in on another North Vietnamese regimental commander when an Arc Light strike began to hit. We suddenly realized where that regiment was located when the enemy commander began to shout for his troops to run east, run east. In about two minutes he was shouting for them to run west, run west. In fact he and his troops were in the middle of the target box and the next load of bombs must have caught them on the wing. There was loud cheering from the battalion's command group when that North Vietnamese commander went off the air. We all knew we had just witnessed an enemy regiment being torn apart and destroyed. The radio operator immediately began another frequency search.

17

The SA-7 Missile Arrives with a Bang

Following a series of ferocious ground attacks during the last week of April, the enemy's pressure against the paratroopers defending the southern outskirts of the town began to slacken. Although the intensity of the ground battle was tapering off, and mortar and artillery attacks had become more sporadic, rounds continued to slam into our position day and night and enemy patrols repeatedly probed our defenses. Their intentions might have been to ensure we were still alert. More likely they were new troops replacing others who had been killed, attempting to confirm the location of our trench line and fighting positions.

Being out and about during the day was not recommended, but it was extremely dangerous to move around after dark because then no one was your friend. In a number of instances enemy snipers climbed into trees during the night so they could see into our perimeter once the sun came up. Cat-and-mouse games became popular with some paratroopers who took on the task of slipping outside the wire to locate and kill them.

Mortar and artillery rounds arrived in the position with little or no warning. The mortar rounds made very little noise before they hit, but the artillery shells usually screamed and moaned on their way in. Even though they often announced their pending arrival, they came in very fast with a terrific explosion that promised serious wounds for soldiers caught out in the open. When mortar or artillery rounds hit trees, steel shrapnel and wood splinters were thrown in all directions. The shrapnel traveled with a terrible velocity. While the wounds from big pieces of shrapnel were dramatic, a very small sliver of steel through the head, heart, or lungs was often less visible but could be equally fatal.

We appreciated the relative respite in the battle's tempo, but we were also sure it was a temporary lull allowing the enemy to reinforce and prepare his next attack. The troops used the time to improve their fighting positions, and they also added more wire entanglements to the rolls of concertina already staked down outside the trench line. Lengths of barbed wire were stretched tight between the stakes and convenient rubber trees, about six inches above the ground. It was crisscrossed back and forth in a maze in front of the rolls of concertina. Hard to see, difficult to crawl under, and almost impossible to run through, tanglefoot was aptly named. We continued sending patrols into the rubber plantation, and every one of them came under fire. The enemy remained directly in front of us, wide awake, and in considerable strength.

Then over a period of several days the intensity of the incoming mortar and artillery fire began to increase, and the enemy kicked off a major ground attack at 4:00 A.M. on 11 May.[1] Under cover of darkness hundreds of North Vietnamese infantry had moved up closer to our trench line. Then, in the midst of a very heavy and very accurate mortar barrage, they rushed us in a full-blown effort to overrun our position. The enemy's infantry assault was full of sound and fury and there was a tremendous amount of small-arms fire. Green tracers seemed to crisscross the position from every direction, some rounds skipping across the ground and others zipping through the trees. Dozens of rocket-propelled grenades flew across the position, smacking into trees with blasts of fire and showers of sparks. There was a constant crash and bang of hand grenades going off inside the position as well as out in the rubber trees. Men were shouting and screaming everywhere. The enemy knew exactly where we were and had orchestrated a major effort to destroy us.

The troops had been preparing for just that eventuality by taking hundreds of grenades out of their individual boxes and stockpiling them ready for immediate use in convenient locations. They had also opened and connected cans of linked machine-gun ammunition in the gun positions, and there were piles of loaded rifle magazines in every fighting position and throughout the length of the trench line. Every man knew his fields of fire and sheets of red tracers cut down enemy infantry while further trimming the rubber trees outside the perimeter. That was the first time I actually heard the enemy use bugles and whistles to control his attack. Hearing those musical signals coming out of the dark in the midst of all the confusion of battle had a direct effect on the paratroopers. It infuriated them. It also helped focus their fire. The soldiers of the 5th Airborne Battalion were intent on delivering bloody murder to their communist enemies.

As the attack unfolded it became clear this was going to be a major effort. I was able to identify several of the enemy's mortar locations and wanted to put air strikes on them as well as on the infantry that was pushing up against our defensive wire. I radioed a situation report to the brigade headquarters in the city and contacted the FAC orbiting over An Loc. The FAC acknowledged my request for air support, but said it would take some time before I would get any help.

While the chain of command in the city had been alerted to the seriousness of our situation, there was no possibility we would get any kind of ground reinforcement because the enemy had unleashed a whole series of attacks at other points around the An Loc perimeter. The North Vietnamese were in the process of conducting a major coordinated push against the city's defenders, and the increased volume of indirect fire we were receiving was being delivered throughout the An Loc area. The intensity of the attack did not diminish with the arrival of daylight, and the enemy continued to feed fresh troops into his ground assault despite suffering extremely heavy casualties. Although the paratroopers in the trenches were well supplied with ammunition and determination, enemy soldiers did succeed in getting through the wire and into the trenches several times during the early morning. Those North Vietnamese were all killed and their bodies thrown out of the position. Friendly casualties were also heavy. The paratroopers were forced to abandon several fighting positions to better consolidate the perimeter.

I had continued talking to the FAC and became more demanding as time went on and no air support had been made available. When the FAC told me all the tactical air had been committed to other missions I really raised my voice, but he still couldn't seem to squeeze any aircraft out of the system for me. By about 7:00 in the morning the battle had begun to stabilize, although the volume of enemy small-arms fire remained very persistent and mortar and artillery rounds continued to slam into the position. The FAC finally radioed to say a team of Cobra gunships would be on station to work for me in a half hour. The Cobras had been providing support farther south on Highway 13, and once rearmed and refueled they would contact me. I was delighted because I still had plenty of targets.

The pilot of the lead Cobra came up on my frequency when the three-ship team was about ten minutes out. He said they had a full load of ammunition and rockets. I remember him saying that he understood we were knee deep in grenade pins. I told him we had a few grenades left, but we also had a lot of targets. He asked me to identify my friendly positions and I explained we were on the south side of the town with friendly troops on both sides of Highway 13. He understood his targets would be farther south of our locations. I also told him I would have a soldier throw a smoke grenade onto the highway to mark our forward positions. It took several minutes to get a soldier positioned to throw the smoke, and when he did the Cobra pilot said he had three colors in sight. That was the clearest indication I ever had that the enemy was listening to my radio transmissions and that he understood everything I was saying. I asked the pilot what the colors were, and when he said one was red I told him that one was mine and everything south of the red smoke was the enemy. I then directed him into the enemy mortar sites and the team of Cobras went to work.

The three helicopters flew a circular pattern, one behind the other. They rolled in on their targets in a steep dive to attack with rockets and miniguns before pulling out to go around for another approach. The targets I'd identified were 200 to 300 yards outside my position and enemy small-arms fire met the Cobras every time they rolled in. They had completed several attacks when, through the uproar and static, I thought I heard one of the pilots transmit, "We're hit, we're hit. We're going in, we're going in."

I was down inside my personal bunker with my radio antenna sticking out the entrance when the pilot shouted his last message, and I stood up to see. For about three seconds I had a clear view through the break in the tree canopy over the bomb crater—the Cobra was about 500 feet above the ground and in a nose-down position, twisting under its main rotor. The tail boom was separated from the body of the helicopter and floating free above it. There was a streak of white smoke in the sky, and a dirty puff where an explosion had torn the tail section completely off the helicopter.

The enemy had fired some kind of missile that had exploded where the engine exhaust was located, and the explosion had been strong enough to tear off the tail section. The pilot didn't transmit again and I dived back into my hole as the aircraft hit the ground well out of sight in the rubber trees.

At first I was not sure exactly what I had seen, but the other Cobra pilots recognized a missile had been fired. One of them had seen it come out of the trees and hit and was sure it was a heat seeker. He thought it was probably an SA-7 shoulder-fired antiaircraft missile. At any rate the pilots of the other Cobras had no intention of continuing their attack, and departed the area. The crew of the downed gunship was lost and we were not able to reach the crash site.[2] While Cobra support disappeared, at least from my part of the battlefield, neither the antiaircraft cannon and machine-gun fire nor the missile threat deterred the fighter planes or AC-130 gunships that piled in during the course of the enemy's frantic attacks on the eleventh. A total of six aircraft were shot down during that day, but 297 fighters and 15 AC-130 gunship sorties participated in turning back the enemy.

After leaving An Loc I learned several pilots had reported seeing SA-7 missiles fired in the vicinity of An Loc as early as mid-April. While those reports had not been officially confirmed, there was absolutely no doubt about

8. AH-1G Cobra helicopters operating over South Vietnam. Photo courtesy of the U.S. Army Aviation Museum.

the SA-7 missile I and those Cobra pilots saw on 11 May. The danger that weapon presented to aircraft over An Loc changed the whole complexion of the battle. For troops on the ground, getting wounded no longer guaranteed a ticket out of the battle. Command and control helicopters from higher head-quarters and the air force FACs all climbed to safer altitudes and the sense of isolation became more compelling for the defenders in An Loc. A compre-hensive list of shot-down aircraft is provided in Appendix 3.

18

To Catch a FAC

Throughout the course of the Easter Offensive the enemy remained focused on overwhelming and destroying the garrison's defenders. Although their initial successes had been stalled, the North Vietnamese were able to orchestrate a series of follow-on attacks that reached a crescendo on 11 and 12 May. It appeared the enemy was throwing all his available reserves into the battle, but his infantry and tank attacks were disjointed and were shot apart and defeated as they appeared. At the same time the enemy poured a truly massive volume of indirect fire into the town. An estimated 7,000 to 8,300 mortar, artillery, and tank main gun rounds impacted in An Loc on the eleventh, and an even greater concentration arrived the following day.[1] That is a crushing weight of shells, and when asked later how the numbers had been tabulated, Colonel Walter Ulmer, the senior advisor to the 5th Army of Vietnam (ARVN) Division and the senior American officer in the city answered: "Counting incoming rounds is an imprecise business. Each ARVN unit was responsible for counting in its own area, and they would total each day in the command bunker. I guess that 7,500 on 11 May is OK, but it may have been a thousand or so more than that, depending on what type you count."

The enemy's ground attacks became more sporadic and less intense the next week, although a few of the surviving enemy were dug in right up against our defensive wire. They were troublesome as they occasionally fired a few rounds or threw grenades into the position, so they had to be located and dealt with. Small teams of soldiers were organized to move out through the wire to find and kill them. The teams went about their job slowly and carefully, crouching and crawling as they searched among the downed trees and litter, under the watchful eyes and shouted directions from their comrades in the perimeter. Progress could be charted by an occasional burst of automatic fire.

Shortly before noon on 14 May I was talking to a FAC about an enemy mortar site I wanted to attack. To get a better view of the target I grabbed my radio and ran to the northern edge of the battalion's battered perimeter, next to the burned-over area. The day was very hot with a few puffy white clouds floating high above in a clear blue sky. As I knelt beside the splintered stump of a rubber tree I could clearly see the FAC's aircraft circling overhead.

The FAC and I were discussing the effectiveness of the attack as he carefully directed each fighter plane into the target. Suddenly, from the edge of some jungle about half a mile to the east, a streak of white smoke shot into the sky. I recognized it was an SA-7 missile. Very fast, it was zooming in a tight spiral toward the FAC. I yelled missile, missile, missile into my handset as it seemed to streak past the FAC's airplane. The airplane flew on for a couple of seconds before I heard a dull boom, and then it began a slow roll to the right. That's when I saw the FAC in the air, falling away from his crippled airplane. He didn't fall very far before his parachute snapped open, and there he was for all to admire, hanging in his parachute harness several thousand feet above the earth.

The FAC had opened his parachute very quickly after he got out of the airplane, which should have given him a lot of time to figure out where he wanted to land, but he just seemed to float until finally disappearing from view some distance to the east of the battalion's perimeter. He was well away from the city or any other friendly troops, but his mind must have been on other things because he just seemed to ride his parachute wherever the fates dictated. His aviator buddies hadn't ignored his plight; another FAC was quickly overhead and several fast-movers were soon making runs and chewing up the jungle to discourage the enemy from getting too close.

Although the FAC had just been unhorsed, it actually turned out to be his lucky day. The battalion's water patrol was down at the creek, generally in the direction his parachute had disappeared. We radioed the patrol leader to look for him. They hadn't seen his parachute and there was no telling if they'd ever find him. Because the missile had been shot from that direction we knew there would soon be a competition with the FAC in the unenviable position of being the prize. But then, within about fifteen minutes we got a call back; the patrol had the FAC and he appeared to be OK. I radioed Colonel Taylor in An Loc to relay the good news to the air force, and within another half hour the returning patrol was approaching the battalion's trench line with the FAC in tow.

Several incoming rounds had smashed into the area in the meantime, and I was back in the security of my hole. I stuck my head out as the patrol filed along the zig-zag path through the defensive wire and saw the FAC when he was about fifty yards away. He was wearing his flight suit and was bare headed. It seemed his helmet had been discarded at some point, although he was clutching a hand-held radio. The FAC was carefully picking his way across the ground, moving slowly and with exaggerated care through the wire. I climbed out of my bunker and waved to attract his attention. He may have glanced up as he came into the position but he was in sensory overload and hadn't focused on me, so I shouted at him. The FAC slammed on the brakes and his head came up like a bird dog as he recognized an American voice. Then he saw me and began to run, picking up steam as he approached. At about fifteen feet he launched and succeeded in delivering a full body tackle. We rolled around on the ground to the vast amusement of the whole battalion, and it took a couple of minutes before he was willing to pry himself loose.

I soon learned my newest best friend was Lieutenant Pep McPhillips, and he had a story to tell. It seemed that after a comfortable night of crew rest and a leisurely and tasty breakfast in the officers' mess he had proceeded to fly around An Loc talking to people like me and bringing dismay and confusion to the enemy. Pep had been transmitting to the fighters and was unable to hear my call when I'd tried to warn him of the missile, so he was totally unprepared when the thing went off just behind his ear. He'd been flying an O-2 Skymaster, a two-seat aircraft with two propellers, one that pulled from the front and another located between the twin booms of the tail, which pushed from behind. Normally there would have been two pilots in the aircraft, but on that day Pep was flying alone and it was probably just as well. The missile came up from behind and zeroed in on the heat signature of the engine exhaust. The explosion tore the tail boom loose and blew out the windshield. The crew compartment was immediately full of wind and confusion, but since there was no one else to get in the way Pep had quickly scrambled around and dived out.

Pep later told me he could not remember pulling the ripcord to activate his parachute. I had to assume he didn't enjoy the freefall sensation because he had certainly been very quick to find that ripcord. And then, after a seemingly endless ride he hit the ground, scratched and shaken but without apparent serious injury although his right ankle was tender. That's when Pep found himself in a brand-new world.

My new FAC friend was a bit disoriented when he finally caught his breath. Not having any idea where to go, he pulled his parachute together and sat on it out of sight under a big elephant ear plant, and waited. Within a few minutes he heard someone walking toward his hiding place. Then a Vietnamese soldier lifted the leaf and smiled at him. None of the soldiers in the patrol spoke English and Pep couldn't speak Vietnamese, so while the paratroopers couldn't communicate effectively they did know who they were looking at. All Pep knew for sure was that he'd been found by Vietnamese soldiers, and it wasn't immediately clear if he'd been rescued or if he was about to start a long hike north to the Hanoi Hilton. Pep later told me he was holding his pistol in one hand and a radio in the other when he was uncovered. Thank goodness he didn't reflexively squeeze off a round because there would have been an immediate and deadly response if a soldier in that hard-bitten and jumpy patrol had gotten winged. Pep also mentioned that several of his saviors immediately whipped out knives and began carving up his parachute, eager to make use of an unexpected but welcome gift.

So Pep joined us in the 5th Airborne Battalion command bunker, but only for a few hours. He enjoyed all the hospitality the house had to offer, including overhead cover and warm creek water liberally laced with iodine purification tablets. The lunch I offered was something of an exciting change from the air force haute cuisine he was no doubt accustomed to. I could tell it took an act of faith on his part to sample some of my favorite fare, rice and mystery meat mixed in an aluminum canteen cup. I'd been hoarding a small can of C-ration peaches, and considering the novelty of a drop-in guest it seemed only appropriate to dig out the can and share. Pep experienced the briefest possible exposure to life in the infantry, but I soon sensed he was not excited about the prospects of staying dirty, unshaven, sweaty, nervous, and bug bitten.

I certainly enjoyed the company of another American, particularly one who was able to bring recent news of the outside world. I could tell I was losing my FAC, however, when he learned the brigade's command bunker in the city had tons of overhead cover rather than the more modest protection the battalion's accommodations could offer. Pep appeared positively anxious to change his address when he realized the bunker in the rubber trees was not his only lodging option. In fact, there was no holding him back even though there was no way for him to leave An Loc and rejoin his squadron until the battle eventually wound down.

I notified Colonel Taylor that Pep and I were going to hike his direction when we got a lull in the action. Even though my FAC had a sore ankle he assured me it would not hold him back and we set off for town a few minutes later. About halfway there we were met by a very intense Vietnamese gentleman on a small two-lung motorbike who had been sent to give Pep a lift. My new air force friend quickly climbed on behind the Vietnamese and off they went in a small cloud of red dust and rackety exhaust as I turned back to rejoin my battalion.

9. An O-2 Skymaster of the type Lieutenant Pep McPhillips flew, affectionately known in the FAC community as the "suck and blow" because of the push and pull propellers. Photo courtesy of Lieutenant Bill Carruthers.

Although Pep had evidenced very little enthusiasm for the more earthy life of an infantryman, I still missed his entertaining company. The fact that he had been able to move on to a more congenial circumstance, and I could not, dampened my spirits for a bit. Our bonding might have been brief, but I still enjoyed listening in from time to time as Pep chatted with his high-flying squadron mates orbiting overhead. I couldn't help but notice, however, that when he exchanged greetings with his air force comrades he always managed to sound a bit abandoned, despite the relative luxury of his accommodations deep in a big, secure bunker in the city.[2]

19

The Helicopter Lifeline Is Cut

During the latter part of April helicopter crews were able to occasionally fly missions into the city, but they were working against an ever more lethal level of enemy fire and they paid the price. American medevac helicopters found it impossible to get close to An Loc after a courageous pickup was accomplished on the south side of town on 3 May.[1] That was a hair-raising mission and to the best of my knowledge it was the last medevac into An Loc until the enemy's grip on the city was eventually broken.

There was no way to evacuate casualties after that point and the wounded either survived or were buried. Poor sanitary conditions, poor diet, and limited medical care all combined to push up the fatality rates. Head, lung, and belly wounds had always been dangerous, but now all kinds of injuries festered quickly and could become fatal. The level of medical care available to soldiers of the battalion consisted of what our surgeon could provide in a bunker in our defensive position while under fire.

It became much more difficult for Cobra gunships to support troops in the vicinity of An Loc after the SA-7 heat seeker was clearly identified on 11 May. I recall one instance a few days later when a Cobra responded to my request for support by firing a load of rockets from altitude and at an extreme standoff distance. The rockets spread out and impacted over a large area and were as dangerous to friendly troops as they were to the enemy. The whole issue became less relevant as the volume of antiaircraft fire continued to increase to the point where helicopters simply could not approach the city and hope to survive. Once it was demonstrated beyond any doubt that the enemy was employing heat-seeking missiles, the rules really changed.

The South Vietnamese army units fighting to reopen Highway 13 were hung up miles to the south, and the Vietnamese air force was tasked to keep the garrison supplied. The aircraft available to accomplish that mission was a squadron of twin-engine C-123 cargo airplanes and a unit of helicopters. The South Vietnamese cargo aircraft had taken a lot of hostile fire and several were shot down attempting to parachute supplies into the city. Although they continued to fly, it was evident the C-123s could not deliver the volume of supplies required and the helicopter unit was ordered to augment their effort by conducting a supply run into the city. The helicopters loaded up and launched their mission the day following the Cobra shoot-down I had witnessed.

The two airborne battalions on the southern outskirts of the city were alerted several hours before the big helicopter supply mission was scheduled to take place. We were told the aircraft would be flying directly up Highway 13 at low altitude to gain some surprise and to hopefully escape heat-seeking missiles. They would be coming right across our positions as they approached the city. We were also told to take cover when they got close because the door gunners would be putting down suppressive fire.

When I heard that cautionary message, I asked the battalion commander to relay to the Vietnamese chain of command that those door gunners should turn off their guns as they approached An Loc. It must have been too hard because at the prescribed hour on the morning of 12 May we heard the helicopters coming up the road. It sounded like every machine gun on every helicopter was firing full blast. The troops immediately crawled as deep as possible into their bunkers.

I peeked out to watch the lead helicopter as it flew across our position. The aircraft was right at treetop level, and I could clearly see the door gunner as he leaned out over his gun, firing wildly into the rubber plantation. I dived back into my hole and began shouting at the brigade senior advisor, Colonel Taylor, on my radio. I told him in no uncertain terms to tell the Vietnamese to turn off the door gunners because they were endangering us. It didn't happen. The whole flight of helicopters roared across the position with all their machine guns firing nonstop. I was furious and let everyone know it. Not only was cowering from friendly fire undignified, the very real possibility of getting hit by a stray bullet from some trigger-happy door gunner really upset me.

The flight of helicopters barreled on into their landing zone, a soccer field in the southern part of town, and immediately threw out their loads. They didn't spend any extra time on the ground before taking off full bore back down Highway 13. The enemy mortar and artillery fire landing in the city certainly hastened them on their way. I later learned they hadn't stayed on the ground long enough to load many of the casualties that had been carried to the soccer field for evacuation. Their departure brought them right back

10. U.S. Army HU-1H helicopter making a high-level approach in the vicinity of An Loc. This photo with a handwritten notation was taken by Warrant Officer Mike Wheeler, courtesy of Carruthers, *The Battle of An Loc: A Massive Convergence of Forces.*

across the battalion's position and once again the door gunners had their machine guns turned on, hosing down everything in sight. Every paratrooper immediately went to ground again, hoping he wouldn't get winged by a stray round. When the last helicopter had departed south we took stock, and much to everyone's surprise not a single man had been hit. A combination of good defensive positions and better luck had ruled the day. The event also demonstrated the ineffectiveness of indiscriminate fire, even when delivered in volume.

With the unsatisfactory conclusion of that effort all attempts to supply the beleaguered city by helicopter came to an end until the siege was broken. While both American and South Vietnamese helicopter units continued to operate well to the south along Highway 13, antiaircraft fire in and around An Loc had become so intense that helicopter missions were simply impossible to accomplish in the vicinity of the town. The supply effort on 12 May confirmed that the Vietnamese air force did not possess the resources required to keep the An Loc garrison alive.

20

The Oldest Lieutenant

While all that was going on, the North Vietnamese persisted in probing our defenses. The battalion also continued to push patrols out into the rubber plantation to demonstrate a bit of aggressive fighting spirit while confirming the location of the enemy. Every patrol went out looking for trouble and succeeded in finding it, and then often came back into the perimeter carrying men who had been wounded or killed. The dead were buried alongside those already interred in our makeshift cemetery. Since the wounded could not be evacuated, they stayed with their buddies to either recover or die. Now that there was no way to get casualties out of An Loc or replacements in, the overall combat effectiveness of the battalion slid even though many of the injured carried on as fighting wounded.

The loss of 51 Company was compounded by the continuing drain on the battalion's foxhole strength. I have a clear mental picture of the moment Colonel Hieu told me he was going to reorganize the battalion and consolidate the surviving soldiers into two full-strength rifle companies. He was not happy about doing a reorganization on the battlefield, but high casualty rates among company officers and sergeants was also creating a command and control problem in the understrength companies. Reorganizing under those conditions had negative historical implications and carried all kinds of potential bad luck, but it had to be done. Colonel Hieu told me the battalion had gone through a similar battlefield reorganization only once before, during the catastrophic battle of Dien Bien Phu in 1954. But the colonel knew he had to act despite the possible bad ju ju, so we tightened up the perimeter and reorganized into a bobtailed battalion of two rifle companies and a tiny headquarters element.

It was during that period the battalion suffered a particularly heavy loss. The oldest lieutenant in the Vietnamese Airborne Division had been a member of the battalion for many years. The day he was killed everyone mourned his loss. The man had started his career as a boy-soldier fighting against the Japanese during World War II. In 1954 he had been a soldier in the Fifth Parachute Battalion, a unit comprised of both Vietnamese and French soldiers that jumped into Dien Bien Phu, not once, but twice—a story in itself. The battalion had been destroyed during that battle, and he had been captured by the Viet Minh. With luck and perseverance he also managed to survive their prison camps.[1] Eventually released by the communists, he then served with Emperor Bao Dai's bodyguard before returning to the Vietnamese army to rejoin his old unit, now designated the 5th Airborne Battalion. Over the years he had been promoted to sergeant major and was eventually commissioned a lieutenant because of his extraordinary experience and leadership qualities. The man had no formal education and knew he would never be promoted beyond the rank of lieutenant, but he had chosen to soldier on until he was killed.

The first and only time I recall seeing the oldest lieutenant was when he was lying on the ground, waiting to be buried. I never knew his name, but I was impressed by how his death, in the midst of a drumbeat of death, affected his fellows. For them, his passing closed a unique and special chapter in the battalion's history. His story was one of lifelong service and total commitment. He hated the communists with a red-hot vengeance and his warrior spirit was the standard his paratrooper brothers aspired to emulate. The oldest lieutenant had been a fierce soldier, and the day a mortar round killed him the rest of us were forced to consider how problematic our own survival was in that terrible place.

21
Belt-Tightening Time

The weather remained very hot with scattered clouds and occasional light rain. Both the volume and accuracy of the enemy's antiaircraft fire had increased steadily during the month of April as aircrews learned to their dismay when two South Vietnamese C-123s and three American C-130s were shot down attempting to parachute supplies to the garrison. It was very dangerous for any kind of aircraft to operate below 9,000 feet as an American AC-130 gunship demonstrated when a heat seeker damaged it on 12 May. The big gunship was able to get home, but at least fifteen aircraft of various types came to grief in the lethal skies during the month of May. By that time the North Vietnamese had established an early warning network of aircraft spotters who were posted on the approaches to the city. When inbound aircraft were sighted the sky was soon filled with antiaircraft fire. Before the battle was over, it was estimated that the North Vietnamese had deployed the equivalent of nine battalions of antiaircraft artillery around An Loc, and the lethality they produced was deadly.

Once it had been clearly demonstrated that the South Vietnamese air force could not deliver the tons of ammunition, food, medical supplies, radio batteries, and the myriad of other items the defenders required, the Americans were tasked to keep the An Loc garrison supplied. The only way the Americans could accomplish that mission was to deliver a large volume of pallets by parachute directly into the city. The story of how the U.S. Air Force responded to that massive job, in this case from the customer's perspective, deserves to be told.

The dire situation faced by the garrison didn't allow air force planners the luxury of spending a lot of time thinking through and preparing for the implications of their new mission. They couldn't wait for the optimum moment when all the desired equipment was ready to go and all the required people were properly trained to start their tasks. The appetite for everything required by the troops defending the city was immense and had to be provided or the garrison would die. The air force started working the problem immediately.[1]

The first American effort to deliver supplies by parachute was conducted on 15 April when a flight of air force C-130s flew straight up Highway 13 from the south. They not only approached the city at well under 1,000 feet, they also came in single file and in the middle of the day. I knew the supply operation was going to take place, but neither I nor anyone else was prepared for how the U.S. Air Force attempted to do it. At the appointed time the first of the C-130s came barreling across our position and on across the city with its back ramp down. Pallets of supplies began appearing over the city, swinging under their enormous cargo parachutes.

The enemy would have exacted a heavier cost on that first transport and its crew, but they were caught by surprise. The North Vietnamese must have been as amazed at the unexpected display of audacity as I was. After that first C-130 droned on out of sight, the enemy quickly recovered and antiaircraft fire began to erupt from all around the city. Green tracers were soon flying up from near and far. The arrival of the second aircraft caused enemy fire to become more intense and much more focused. That C-130 was shot full of holes, the navigator was killed, and two other crewmembers were wounded as the load was delivered. The pilots managed to get the aircraft back to Tan Son Nhut despite an on-board fire, but after that harrowing experience the problem had to be rethought.

A day later the C-130s were back. That time they came in from all different directions to unload their cargos over the city. They arrived at treetop level and popped up over the southern part of An Loc to give the cargo parachutes time to open once the pallets had been pushed out the back of the aircraft. As soon as their loads were clear the C-130s quickly dived back down to escape the antiaircraft fire as they dodged away from the city. The accuracy of those deliveries was not good and very few of the parachute loads could be recovered, and aircraft were still hit in the process. One was so shot-up it was forced to crash land south of the city. Luckily the crew was rescued by a pair of helicopters whose pilots had seen the crash. All the crews had made a courageous effort, but that method of delivery was not the solution either.

The next iteration had the C-130s climb above the effective range of the ground fire and parachute the pallets from 9,000 feet. The parachutes were on static lines and opened immediately after leaving the aircraft. Even when ground winds were light there were other winds at different levels up to the drop altitude. That made it difficult to calculate an accurate exit point for the drop and parachutes drifted far and wide. Some were recovered, but many were beyond the reach of friendly locations and given up to the enemy. The percentage of recovered pallets was very low, and serious questions were raised about the ability of the South Vietnamese defenders to maintain their cohesion and their will to fight on those diminished levels of supply.

The high-level parachuting technique was then refined by employing a system known as High Altitude/Low Opening (HALO). Under this plan the pallets would still be dropped at an altitude beyond the effective range of the enemy's antiaircraft fire. The loads would initially fall several thousand feet while stabilized by small drogue parachutes. At a pre-set altitude an automatic opening device would activate the big cargo parachutes, and hopefully the result would be an accurate delivery of supplies to the troops waiting below. The system might have shown promise on other occasions, but the results were not auspicious in this instance. The first HALO drop was flown on 4 May. Some loads missed the town and several other pallets streamered in when their parachutes failed to open. Bags of rice and ammunition crates slammed into the ground in a roar of dust and flying debris. In one case a pallet smashed a bunker flat, killing the people inside. It was time to reconsider and another supply halt was called.

The next version had the C-130s flying back up Highway 13, but this time at night. The air force wanted the troops on the ground to mark the drop zone although no one in An Loc was anxious to get out in the open to light fires. In fact there was so much confusion in the city it would have been very difficult for aircrews to separate out any markers the defenders might have been able to generate from other fires on the ground. Weather conditions remained generally clear during that period, and the city was plainly visible from the air. Everyone agreed the prominent soccer field in the southern half of town should remain the primary drop zone. The defenders assured the air force that pallets would be recovered if they landed anywhere close to the drop zone.

When the first aircraft arrived to attempt a low-level night drop, the enemy was much more prepared and a cyclone of green tracers erupted from all around the city. Aircraft braved that gauntlet of fire several nights, but with mixed results, and that option was also canceled. Everyone on the ground pulled up their belts another notch; they were going to get hungrier. They also recognized it was essential to conserve ammunition. The air force planners regrouped to consider another method of getting supplies to the garrison.

A technique was finally developed that provided an excellent balance between getting the needed supplies to the troops while providing an accept-

able level of protection for the aircraft and their crews. The successful solution was to go back to 9,000 feet, but now large drogue parachutes were
attached to each pallet rather than the standard cargo parachutes.

Those drogue parachutes did not have the typical solid canopies of conventional parachutes. Instead, they were slotted. They looked like they had
been constructed using strips of material that allowed some of the air normally held inside the canopy to escape, while still stabilizing their loads in
the air. Although the loads came in fast, troops on the ground had time to
get out of the way. The drops could be made during daylight hours so the air
crews could clearly see their intended drop zone. That system allowed the air
crews to calculate their drop points with greater accuracy, and the defenders
began to collect an ever-larger volume of supplies.

The drops were conducted on a schedule so the troops could be prepared
to collect the loads as they were delivered. It took days for this final and successful method of supply delivery to get worked out, but once it was per-
fected the volume of materials delivered increased rapidly. Supply rates soon
began to more closely match the requirements of the defending troops. That
was a most welcome development for everyone in An Loc because then some
of the tightened belts could actually be relaxed a notch or two. We stopped
trying to conserve ammunition and began to receive plenty of fresh batteries for our radios. Our diets also improved when carrying parties began returning from the city with sacks of rice and an occasional case of C-rations
to split up and share among the troops.

As the operation matured, fewer of the pallets drifted beyond the reach
of the defenders. Just knowing that friendly troops would recover most of
what we could see coming out of the C-130s was a big morale boost. Aerial
supply missions were identified by the term Santa Claus, and when our radio
announced those welcome words we knew more of what we needed was on
the way. Getting supplies onto the ground and inside the garrison's perimeter
was a big step forward, but the enemy continued to pound the city with artillery and mortar fire, and gathering up those supplies once they were on the
ground was still a daunting job. The soldiers who worked to unload pallets
labored in a place of extreme danger. Men were routinely injured or killed
as they pulled the nylon webbing off loads.

Another part of the supply problem was to ensure that materials were effectively distributed once they were recovered. The issue centered on getting
specific kinds of things to the troops who needed those things most. What
often happened was less than professional; the troops who first got to the
prize sometimes insisted they owned the pallet and everything tied to it. In
an environment of increasing scarcity, many weren't willing to simply give

12. A customer's view of a C-130 aircraft delivering supplies. Photo courtesy of the U.S. Air Force.

valuable things away. They would, however, trade for items they needed that had been recovered from other pallets. That more informal practice of supply distribution opened the door to all kinds of conflict and abuse. Several shoot-outs between competing groups attempting to grab a treasure added to an already deadly level of tension among the defenders.

Meeting the supply requirements of the various units in An Loc was uneven, wasteful, and unsatisfactory, and the process remained chaotic even after Colonel Luong, the airborne brigade commander, was put in charge of fixing the problem. He laid down the law, but his efforts were subverted at every turn by soldiers who hoarded, sold, and traded at the wholesale level. Even the aluminum pallets were valuable as they could be quickly incorporated into the construction of bunkers and fighting positions. While a pallet wouldn't provide much protection by itself, it made a great roof to load with sandbags and bricks for overhead cover.

Because both the 5th and the 8th Airborne Battalions were located outside the city's perimeter, the supply distribution problem was presented to us in clear and unambiguous terms. Getting materials out to the battalions, or

13. An airdrop coming into An Loc. Photo by Colonel Walter
Ulmer, courtesy of Carruthers, *The Battle of An Loc: A Massive
Convergence of Forces.*

even making a visit to the brigade's command bunker on the southern edge
of town, meant a hazardous hike through shot and shell. Carrying parties
were leery because of the dangers involved, but we had to get the essentials
and only had the one source of supply. Despite an increase in the number of
pallets recovered, air-delivered food remained scarce in the battalion. An occasional C-ration meal with the boiled rice became an event.

Our jungle water supply remained accessible, but I knew it had to be badly
contaminated and I religiously added plenty of iodine purification tablets to

each canteen of water in an effort to stay healthy. So while there was enough water to drink, regardless of its questionable source, my diet was meager. It consisted largely of boiled soups containing rice and various parts of a cow that had ventured too close to the battalion perimeter. Bits and pieces of local vegetable matter were also included. It all became part of the daily diet no matter how unappetizing in appearance or taste.

Short rations combined with the generally unsavory living conditions resulted in a number of soldiers getting sick, including me. For the first and only time in my life I began to suffer from some kind of dysentery, and it got serious. I found myself squatting about every three hours and sometimes more often, day and night. The constant loss of liquid began to take its toll. As a result I went from a healthy and energetic 185 pounds to a 140-pound anemic and agitated shadow of my former self. I spent a lot of time dreaming of beer and steak, cherry pie and ice cream. I longed for the canned fruit that came in C-rations, but all those prospects were equally problematic where I lived. My stomach had actually shrunk to the point where I wouldn't have been able to eat a full meal if one had suddenly appeared before me.

I also learned that being worn down to such an extent affected every aspect of my miserable existence, including my patience and general outlook on life. My normal sense of optimism began to fade as I got weaker. I couldn't find anything funny about the demands of self-preservation that became more urgent with every passing day. I seemed to lose whatever appetite I had when food was available, and forced myself to eat without comment or interest. I didn't have the energy to carry on long conversations. I was irritated about almost everything and took the greatest satisfaction in attacking and killing the cause of all my discomforts at every opportunity. I slept when I could.

Conditions for all the troops in An Loc continued to be very grim with massive artillery attacks interspersed with North Vietnamese ground attacks; there was no let-up in sight. The enemy's major effort to split the An Loc perimeter on 11 and 12 May succeeded in driving two wedges into the city's defenses, one on the western side of town and the other in the northeastern corner.[2] The South Vietnamese had been able to keep the enemy's attacks from linking up in the middle of town, and after hard fighting the western salient was recaptured. But after almost a week the defenders had not been able to retake the ground lost in the northeastern part of town, and the 5th Airborne Battalion's phone rang.

We were ordered to conduct a hasty attack to destroy that persistent threat to the garrison's integrity. We got the mission because we were smaller than the 8th Airborne Battalion. The brigade commander, Colonel Luong, took a calculated risk and decided we could generate enough combat power to do the job in town. Our sister battalion's soldiers would have to dig their heels in deeper and cover the southern approaches to An Loc by themselves.

It certainly didn't take long to pack up. We'd recently completed eating the last part of the unfortunate cow and were encouraged that our supply line into town was going to get shorter. The 8th Airborne Battalion was left alone when we pulled out on 17 May. Those unyielding but hard-pressed paratroopers continued to battle the enemy and block the southern approach into the city until Highway 13 was finally reopened.

As our portion of the battle had progressed and casualties continued to mount, the forlorn battalion cemetery had also expanded. I don't know how many soldiers had been buried by the time we left that position, but the battalion commander made a point of saluting their ranks as we departed. Every dead paratrooper's place was identified by a wooden marker driven into the ground. Each marker had a piece of paper with the soldier's name and home of record inscribed, and helmets protected the messages from the elements. Those men had been buried by a couple of their buddies; each one put into the ground with little or no ceremony. It was just too dangerous to stay out in the open for long, even for a final good-bye. An increasing number of soldiers in our thinning ranks were bandaged, and some had serious wounds, but I never saw a shirker during that period of incredible stress and privation.

The bravery and fortitude of those Vietnamese paratroopers surpassed anything I had ever experienced. There was no possibility of relief and no good outcome in sight, and they just cleaned their weapons and focused on the job at hand. At the same time my personal view of the world had become narrower and grimmer, and I was ready for a change of address even if it meant lugging my gear into a tougher part of town. When the order was given to move, the troops pulled their equipment together and climbed out of their decaying fighting positions. They quickly formed up into a loose tactical formation and began the short march into An Loc. The battalion was visibly smaller, but even so it was a disciplined unit comprised of the toughest and most professional soldiers I could ever hope to see.

We were all filthy. We hadn't washed in weeks and the red grit was thoroughly ground into skin, clothing, and equipment. When not wet and clinging, the clay in the fighting positions and bunkers had the consistency of talcum powder, or finely pulverized dust. It found every crease and wrinkle and moving part, particularly when mixed with sweat or gun oil. My hair was getting shaggy and was stiff and matted with dirt. There was no way to stay clean and everyone had taken on a dull brick hue. The Vietnamese smelled of sweat, fish oil, and explosives, and I'm sure they found me equally un-appetizing. I didn't have any trouble working my slide-action shotgun, and the troops had stayed busy cleaning their automatic weapons and the belts of linked machine-gun ammunition to preclude jams. The sun was bearing down, the sweat was running, and shell fire was impacting several places in the city as we trudged toward the An Loc meat grinder.

22
Moving Uptown

It was a half-strength battalion that set about girding its loins for the next task. I didn't have time to meet with the 8th Airborne Battalion advisors across the road, but I did have a brief radio discussion with that battalion's senior advisor, Lieutenant Winston Cover, to be sure he knew we were pulling out. They planned to out-post our old position and we were ready to go in less than an hour after getting the brigade order. The claymore mines were left in place for the use of our airborne brothers, but we took all the small-arms ammunition and grenades we could carry. Our two reorganized rifle companies were up to strength, but there were only the two of them. It was a poignant moment when we turned our backs on our unit dead to take on our new mission.

The battalion command group, consisting of a half dozen men, fell in between the two companies as the troops left their fighting positions. Standing near the entrance of my hole-in-the-ground bunker, I noticed one in every three or four of the soldiers moving past was bandaged. Some of the wounds appeared superficial but some were serious. Those wounded who couldn't walk were being carried by their buddies, some on stretchers and others slung in ponchos tied to poles. The men were filthy from living in the ground, and they were hungry and anemic from skimpy rations. Overloaded with weapons and extra gear recovered from the dead, they were nervous and jumpy and they stayed close to cover when they moved. There was no talking or laughing as they peered from under the lips of their steel helmets. They were keyed up and ready to shift from defense to attack at the slightest provocation. Battle-hardened, the surviving soldiers of the 5th Airborne Battalion were a tough and dangerous crew.

In one sense I was relieved to depart the smashed and littered position in the rubber trees. I was more than ready to get out of the cramped bunker and the dirt I'd been living in. But regardless of any upside to the move, I still had to take a deep breath as I looked around. Leaving the relative safety of my hole in the red earth forced me out into the open, and I felt unprotected and vulnerable. While we didn't receive any effective small-arms fire as we approached An Loc, a few bullets went zipping past. Enemy mortar and artillery rounds continued to impact in and around the town. Occasionally I wouldn't hear any weapons firing or any explosions for several minutes at a time, but then it would start again. The sounds of war were always there and the dangerous effects could not be ignored.

The soldiers were well spread out as we left the fractured rubber plantation. We soon crossed the open area and found ourselves moving into a welter of urban destruction. My first impression was the whole place had been wrecked, knocked apart, and abandoned. Roofs were torn off buildings, walls were blasted apart, and tumbled, burned-out cars and trucks lay in scorched spots on the streets. Splintered tree stumps poked through the rubble, litter and clutter was blown everywhere. Pieces of furniture from homes and offices, scraps of clothing and paper, and sheets of twisted metal roofing littered the streets. Traces of smoke from smoldering fires and the stink of explosives blanketed the whole city.

An Loc had been smashed by the enemy's massive artillery attacks and looked like old newsreels of war-torn towns I remember seeing as a kid. A few of the soldiers defending the southern edge of town stuck their heads out of basement windows as we moved past. They did not appear happy when they began to realize there were now fewer friendly troops between them and the aggressive enemy.

Initially I was most impressed by the destroyed structures, but then I began to see the bodies. Dead soldiers, civilians, cows, pigs, chickens, and things I couldn't identify were lying in the street or partially buried in the rubble. The thick cloying green stink of the decaying dead permeated everything. As I became more attuned I began to see dirt mounds beside buildings that marked temporary graves. I also recognized the remains of bodies that had been blown out of their graves by the incessant artillery fire. Staying close to cover I had to step across bodies that had been thrown up against the foundations and the walls of buildings. I could see others sprawled in gutted alleyways and blasted-out storm drains. Many of the dead must have been in the open for weeks as they were shriveled black by the sun, their juices soaking into the masonry fragments and dirt.

As we got deeper into the town, the destruction seemed to get worse. Every building was badly damaged and most were destroyed. Everything that had been in them was blown all over the area. We soon walked by the first of sev-

eral destroyed T-54 tanks we encountered that day. It was burned out and a
broken track had run off into the street, released from its drive sprocket. The
crew was still aboard and the rotting bodies, the burned vehicle, and the oil
and grease on the shattered pavement combined to produce a gagging stink.
The battalion had to stop several times so commanders could get their bearings in that wasteland of destruction.

We intended to go directly into the attack to recapture the ground that had
been lost, but it took some time to coordinate our move through the South
Vietnamese units in the area. There didn't seem to be a coherent perimeter
defense to orient on, although we did find soldiers defending strong points. It
was hard to get a clear picture of the situation on the ground, and we didn't
want any confusion with friendly troops as we began our attack. Artillery
shells were impacting in the city and smoke and dirt were drifting in the stifling air. At one point I recall kneeling on the ground with Colonel Hieu and
the two company commanders. We had taken refuge between partially de-
molished concrete walls as we attempted to match up landmarks on a city
map with the smashed neighborhoods we were looking at. After studying the
map and scanning the surrounding area, the Vietnamese officers glanced at
me and shook their heads as if to say now we're in the serious stuff. One of
the company commanders grinned and pointed at a wrecked jeep that had
been blown onto the roof of a partially destroyed two-story building. It was
upside down and embedded in the shattered rafters and tiles, and I remember thinking it must have taken a really big shell to throw it that high.

As we began to move again I stepped around the corner of a wall to discover a smashed-up public latrine. The brick structure had been partially
blown down, and glancing in I saw the remains of several bodies floating
face down in a pit of brown soup. It was terribly hot in the direct sun and the
sweat was running. The flies were fat and sticky and they were everywhere
and insistent. The whole place was putrid and foul, and it was very dangerous
to be out in the open. The troops were anxious to keep moving. They wanted
to get on with the job and under cover.

Each of the companies was responsible for clearing the enemy from an
area roughly two blocks wide and about five blocks deep, although it was
hard to tell precisely given the destruction. The direction of attack and the
final objectives were pointed out to the company officers, and the battalion
went directly into the attack. Machine-gun teams laid down a base of fire and
the troops charged across the street that was the battalion's line of departure.
They were wearing their rucksacks and were loaded down with ammunition.
The wounded had been collected in the basement of an abandoned building,
and the surplus gear was left in piles to deal with later.

The enemy was simply not prepared to face the ferocity of the 5th Airborne Battalion. Working in teams, the paratroopers threw grenades into rooms and over walls and followed the explosions with a rush and blast of automatic fire. Company officers and sergeants coordinated their troops as they advanced through the destroyed buildings and rubble-strewn neighborhoods. The companies succeeded in recapturing the first two blocks of the salient by sundown, but the troops needed ammunition so Colonel Hieu ordered them to consolidate where they were. The command group went to ground in a vegetable patch in someone's back yard.

Soldiers who had been badly wounded were carried back to our surgeon's improvised aid station. The carrying parties then returned to their companies with the required ammunition and cans of water. The half dozen paratroopers killed in the attack were collected and buried in shallow graves along the base of a wall inside a schoolyard. North Vietnamese were left where they died. The battalion had not taken any prisoners.

I coordinated with the FAC for tactical air strikes to support the night attack, which was ready to kick off at 10:00 P.M. Flares of one type or another were constantly burning over the city, and combined with fires on the ground there was plenty of light for the attack. I remember being impressed by the amount of illumination and how well I could see as we began to move. Visibility at night in the town was much better than it had ever been under the rubber trees.

The air strikes went in on schedule, and I later adjusted the fires of an AC-130 gunship to support one of the companies having trouble taking a large building. The directed fires from Spectre provided the punch we needed, and well before daylight both rifle companies had fought their way to the cross street marking the battalion's limit of advance. Once our objectives were secured we coordinated with units on our flanks, and the troops dug in to defend our portion of the An Loc perimeter.

The command group moved into a small but conveniently located bunker that had been constructed during a former time. Built in the middle of a large intersection, its cramped size was offset by the fact that it was fort-like. Ten feet across and six feet deep, the bunker was capped with layers of wooden railroad ties, steel rails, and dirt that totaled about four feet of good overhead cover. There were narrow firing ports on every side, allowing the occupants to see out in all directions right at ground level. It was reassuring to know we could cover the streets feeding into the intersection with grazing fire if the need arose. Even though it was a tight fit for the command group, we all moved in with a sigh of relief. That thick roof gave great comfort in a world dominated by unexpected rude surprises.

I was carrying my radio in my rucksack and using a short antenna since most of my conversations were with the FAC flying somewhere overhead. The longer whip antennas on the battalion commander's radios were initially stuck out the door of the bunker. They were soon clipped off by shrapnel and the operators were kept busy rigging improvised wire antennas that had to be repaired periodically.

Our battalion surgeon was a brave and intelligent man who had been educated in France. He had served with the battalion for several years and spent most of his time tending to the seriously wounded in his various improvised aid stations. The day after we moved into An Loc he was hit in the head by a steel splinter and died while helping carry a wounded paratrooper to cover. Even though our medical supplies had been scanty for weeks, his presence had been very reassuring and losing him was a serious development. The surgeon's death was yet another reminder that the Grim Reaper was with us and that his touch could be indiscriminate—and sudden.

We heard there were enemy artillery observers loose in the city, adjusting North Vietnamese artillery onto targets they could identify. I initially discounted that bit of news as unlikely given the volume of fire that continued to pour in, equally dangerous to all who might be moving around. But I had to reconsider when a pair of enemy artillery pieces began to systematically search for our bunker. The first afternoon we were in residence a pair of really big artillery shells came screaming in from north of town to smack into the middle of the street about fifty yards out in front of us. About fifteen minutes later two more rounds came roaring in to explode down the street to our rear.

We had noticed the first two rounds, but the next two really got everyone's undivided attention when they seemed to bracket our bunker. In another fifteen minutes they were followed by two more exploding across the intersection to our front. After the time required for another adjustment, two more rounds came whistling in to blast a building on the other side of the street, throwing bricks and steel shrapnel in all directions. In every instance the two rounds came in together, and we could pick them out of the background noise because of their uniformity and size. They were really big. The blast and concussion was extreme and caused us to crouch in the bottom of the bunker and grit our teeth. The guns must have been sitting right next to each other. The rounds came in parallel, riding a flat trajectory, and given the nature of their target we took them personally. They were seriously scary.

It didn't take me long to get on my radio to the overhead FAC with a description of our situation. He had already been looking for enemy artillery positions north of the city, and I tried to narrow his search to find the guns shooting at my bunker. I gave him my best reading of the magnetic azimuth marking the shell's track, although I couldn't be absolutely sure with all the weapons and radios in the bunker pulling at the north-seeking arrow. Despite his encouragement I wasn't ready to climb atop the bunker to get a better reading. Over the next several hours the FAC directed a series of air attacks onto likely targets, but the two guns continued to fire. While the rounds always hit close together, their impact points seemed to wander around the area. Either the enemy gunners were not computing their data accurately or the adjustments they were receiving were not very precise. Even so, sheets of high-velocity shrapnel periodically thumped and smacked into the sandbags and wooden timbers on the outside of our bunker, causing dirt to trickle out of the roof and onto the bodies hunkered down inside.

The size and persistence of those incoming shells spurred us to dig a six-foot deep, X-shaped trench into the bunker's dirt floor as an additional precaution. Only the battalion commander refrained from getting his hands dirty, but when it was finished he was quick to join us in the new trench. That's where we stayed for some additional protection should the bunker take a direct hit and the railroad ties and rails get blasted in on top of us. The big artillery rounds continued to come screaming in about every fifteen minutes, exploding someplace in the immediate vicinity, and we continued to sweat.

Then, after what seemed like hours, the shelling stopped ripping into the neighborhood. Everyone in the bunker heaved a big sigh of relief when it seemed the ordeal was over, hoping the guns had been killed by an air strike. I was certainly glad to disentangle myself from the intimacy of the sweat-soaked paratroopers in the bottom of that stifling and stinking trench, and the radio operators slipped outside to repair their antennas.

That night I took occupancy of the X-shaped trench because no one else wanted to sleep there, and it actually gave me a bit of room to stretch out. About three in the morning another pair of big shells came screaming right at us to explode in the street immediately in front of the bunker, slamming pulverized concrete and steel splinters into the outside walls. I had just enough time to jackknife into a corner before everyone piled back in. We decided the two guns had probably stopped firing because they had used up their ready supply of ammunition, but now they had been replenished and were back in action. The next two rounds arrived right on time, and they continued to impact with terrifying regularity. Colonel Hieu acted like he was getting ready to make a run for it, but it was dark and he didn't have a clear idea where he wanted to go anyway, so we gritted our teeth as the shells continued to search for our stifling but well-protected hole in the ground.

About ten pairs of those massive shells arrived over the next hours and

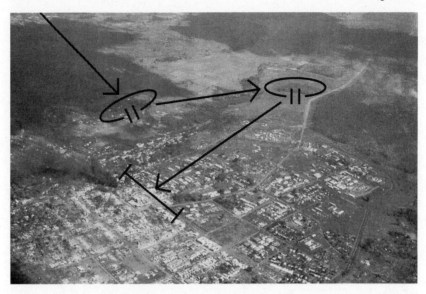

14. The 5th Airborne Battalion's movement into An Loc on 17 May is depicted by the arrow in the center of the photo, courtesy of Lieutenant Bill Carruthers.

several were close enough to deafen everyone and fill the bunker with smoke and dirt. It was totally dark in the bottom of the trench where we crouched with our knees pulled up and our helmets pulled down. My nose and mouth were full of dirt and the very strong copper taste of heart-thumping fear. As I wrapped my arms around my knees I tried to imagine something pleasantly distracting, but waiting for the next pair of incoming rounds and the blast and concussion followed by dirt shaking out of the roof and running down my shirt demanded total concentration. It was simply not possible to take a mental trip and escape the reality of that place. The serious injury or death that would arrive with a direct hit caused everyone to sweat and mutter. There wasn't any room in my brain for anything but those shells as I waited for the catastrophe that would bring the bunker down into the hole. At one point one of the soldiers began to groan and sob, which caused the operations officer to slap him hard and tell him to be quiet. But then the enemy gun crews must have run out of ammunition again because the shelling stopped.

We all crouched in the bottom of the trench until just before daylight, blinking at one another and dozing periodically. Some of those rounds had hit very close, and in the partial light of dawn Colonel Hieu said it was time to go. He insisted on moving into the basement of a nearby house that had been checked out by the radio operators. I grabbed my rucksack and shotgun and scrambled outside when it was my turn, but then I took a look at several of the shell holes. Rounds that had hit in the hard-topped street had blown dish-shaped impressions a foot deep and several feet across. I confirmed the shells had come from north of the city as the dirt and shrapnel spray was out the south sides of the holes. A number of shells had hit within twenty feet of the bunker and several were right up against the walls. No wonder they had rattled our teeth. If the immediate past was any indicator, the North Vietnamese gunners would have another load of ammunition in a few hours and would begin firing again. The odds ensured that a round would eventually hit the bunker and it was time for us to move into less identifiable, and hopefully less stressful, quarters.

We searched for but never uncovered any North Vietnamese artillery observers in the city. Although we didn't find them, I knew they were there. They had tried their level best to bury me in that miserable bunker, but they failed.

23
Sick Call in the Basement

The battalion command group relocated into the filthy basement of a two-story house fifty yards down the street from our cramped and beleaguered bunker. We got to our new abode by running down a back alley, and arrived in an adrenalin-pumping rush with rucksacks and weapons banging against doorframes as we piled down the stairs. The house fronted directly onto the street that marked the northeastern corner of the An Loc perimeter and we soon discovered the enemy was barricaded in the buildings right across the street. There was an intermittent exchange of gunfire between the paratroopers in the house above us and the enemy thirty yards away.

Our new command post was a concrete cellar with a low ceiling and crumbling walls. It was a dark and dingy place, divided into two rooms. There were several small grills in the outside walls that let in a bit of fresh air, although those facing the street were jammed with bricks to keep grenades out. While the unobstructed grills allowed some light during the daytime, we still had to use flashlights to read our maps or change the frequencies on our radios. One of the dim and odorous rooms had been used as a latrine by a group of civilians who were occupying the place when we moved in. Looking bedraggled and thoroughly subdued, they consisted of a variety of the elderly, a dozen children of various ages, and a hugely pregnant woman. We moved the civilians into the room they had been using as their latrine and got ourselves organized on the less disgusting side of the dividing wall.

The roof of the house had been partially destroyed but the floor above us was a poured concrete slab so we were happy with the overhead protection. Our basement also served as the kitchen for soldiers in residence upstairs, and they came and went at all hours of the day and night. The battalion aid station had been set up in another building a block behind us. Only the most seriously wounded were collected there, although in several cases men were carried into our basement before they could be directed on to the aid station.

Early one morning a badly wounded soldier was helped down the stairs and laid on the floor by several of his buddies. He had been hit in the lower arm days before and had insisted on staying with his squad, but had become so sick his friends decided to get help. They knew the battalion surgeon had been killed and hoped Colonel Hieu could do something for their friend. When the bandages came off a smell of rotting meat blossomed and filled the room. Colonel Hieu took a look and called me over. I found myself examining something I had read about but never actually seen before. There didn't seem to be much bleeding, but the whole area around the seeping wound was swollen and discolored. The soldier's hand and forearm had ballooned to an enormous size and the shiny skin was stretched tight and looked ready to split. Angry red streaks ran up inside the man's arm to his armpit, another symptom of gangrene I remembered reading about.

I thought the soldier would probably die if the arm didn't come off, and that's what I told Colonel Hieu. His response was he wished the surgeon hadn't been killed, and I certainly agreed. Since there was no possibility of evacuating anyone out of An Loc, Colonel Hieu wanted to know if I could do the job. He didn't want to move the soldier to a primitive medical holding area near the soccer field and we both knew an amputation was well beyond the confidence level of our unit medics. I was equally untrained when it came to something as serious as major surgery, but as I looked around that squalid basement for some alternative I knew if I didn't try to help the man he wouldn't get helped.

I did have one encouraging thought as I considered options and sought inspiration. I recalled reading that thousands of men had suffered amputations during the American Civil War with no anesthesia and under conditions not so very different from what we were experiencing. I told Colonel Hieu I thought I could do it, and he had a soldier run to the battalion aid station for the surgeon's medical kit. Once the kit arrived I went through it and was disappointed to find that except for some pressure bandages there wasn't much that would be helpful.

My new patient was small and skinny and probably didn't weigh more than 120 pounds. There was no way to knock him out, but he was drifting in and out of consciousness and I figured he'd probably faint once I went to work, providing his heart didn't just stop beating. Although streaks of infection ran up to his shoulder I didn't want to try to amputate his arm that high because I didn't have a saw to cut through the bone of his upper arm. I thought it would be best to separate his elbow joint. I was afraid that amputating his arm at the elbow might be too low to stop the infection, but I also figured I could cut through that joint with a sharp knife. I knew trying to take his arm off at the shoulder was much too complicated to consider and I didn't want to get into the middle of something I couldn't finish.

Even though there were several light-weight scalpels in the surgeon's kit I decided to use my heavy bladed K-Bar knife. It was sharp and I could get a good grip on the leather handle, plus I could press down on the flat top of the blade if more pressure was needed. I didn't feel comfortable trying to use the thin scalpels. There wasn't any way to sterilize his arm or my hands or my knife, so it didn't take long to get ready. Colonel Hieu refused to participate but the radio operators held flashlights. I tied a very tight tourniquet around my patient's upper arm and when everyone seemed prepared I told his buddies to hold him down. I gripped his wrist tight, took a deep breath, and made a strong cut across the inside of his elbow. He groaned and kicked and tried to get free but his buddies held tight and I continued to cut. The arm didn't bleed much but the tendons and ligaments were tough and it took a lot of pressure to cut through and find the joint. At one point it didn't seem like the elbow was going to separate and I couldn't see what was holding it together, so I just leaned on the knife and finished the job.

It probably took about ten minutes to get the arm off and wrap the stump in a wad of cotton and a length of bandage. I loosened the tourniquet a bit and then took it off when the stump didn't bleed through the bandage. I don't know what happened to the amputated arm but I do know that my patient was totally unconscious when the job was finally finished.

The sweat was running off me like a river, and I felt a bit queasy as I sat on my helmet and considered what I'd just done. The smell of fresh blood added a new layer to the odors in the grubby basement, and I was relieved when the soldier's buddies carried him away to the aid station. I knew there was very little that could be done for him there, but he had to be moved out of the command post. Once my one-armed patient was out of sight, I found a canteen of water and washed the blood off my hands and cleaned my knife.

What I discovered about myself that morning was that I had become almost totally desensitized to the pain and distress of others. While the smell of fresh blood on the concrete floor had begun to turn my stomach, actually cutting the man's arm off had only been an unwelcome job I took on because I thought it was necessary and no one else would do it. My patient survived several days. I thought he probably died because the infection had progressed too far to stop without the massive doses of antibiotics we didn't have. That, plus his diminished physical condition, didn't allow him to survive.

The shelling of the city continued day and night, but our protected command post shielded us from much of the sound as well as the destruction of the incoming rounds. Early one morning, however, the realities of living in an impact area were suddenly brought back into focus for all of us. I was sitting on my helmet with my back against one of the flaking concrete walls when a totally unexpected and truly tremendous explosion knocked me off my seat. As my head began to clear I found myself lying on the floor, curled up in a fetal position with my hands pressed against the sides of my head. The basement was full of dust and I couldn't hear anything. My head felt like someone had slammed me hard with a pair of boards. Blood was seeping out of my ears and as I lay on the floor the fuzzy deafness slowly became a high-volume whine in my head that seemed to accelerate the pain.

I let go of my head and rolled over onto my hands and knees to look around. Through the pain and confusion I could see everyone in the room was on the floor, either curled up and holding their heads or sprawled out unconscious. A slow and detailed examination of my various body parts indicated nothing was broken or missing. I finally realized an artillery shell had come into the building and exploded on the concrete floor immediately over our heads. It hadn't penetrated the basement, but the concussion in that confined space had been terrific. I recall a lieutenant coming down the stairs to check on the battalion commander after he replaced the soldiers who had been killed or wounded in the house above us.

The civilians on the other side of the basement were screaming and moaning. The explosion had a particularly dramatic effect on the pregnant woman and her baby. In fact, it seemed the baby had decided to make an immediate appearance. The mother-to-be announced the pending arrival with a series of soul-wrenching screams that began to build in both frequency and tempo. All the Vietnamese men, civilians and soldiers alike, were terrified of her predicament and wouldn't have anything to do with her. The elderly women seemed to be totally confused and helpless. All the Vietnamese refused to get close to her and the shouts and screams were rapidly becoming more insistent. In addition to never previously doing major surgery, I had also never delivered a baby. The woman sounded like she was in extremis so I eventually decided to see if anything could be done to stop the intensifying shrieks.

She was on her back on the littered floor with her knees up, and she was pressing both hands against her belly. Her mouth was wide open and she was howling like a wolf. I'm sure under normal conditions she would have been terribly upset to have a strange white man see her in such a situation, but at that moment she was well past caring about me, so I took a look. I could actually see the slicked black hair on the top of the kid's head, and then its ugly little face appeared with a pop. I grabbed its head and pulled. For a moment there was some resistance and I was afraid its head might come off in my hand, but then the whole baby suddenly slid right out like a little wet slug. There was a gush of water and blood, and I grabbed the slippery little thing before it could hit the floor. A quick inspection told me it was a he. I'd read that a doctor might have to hold up a newborn by its feet and slap its bottom to make it cry and start its breathing, but I didn't get to try that part of the procedure. He started squealing and snorting almost immediately and seemed fully prepared to get on with the business of life without any encouragement from me. His wretched mother had stopped yelling, and she grabbed the baby away from me just as she pushed a load of blood and placenta out onto the floor. It was time for me to retreat to my side of the basement. I decided to let her worry about umbilical cords and any other housekeeping duties that might be indicated. Although the assistance I had given the woman was met with a mixed response by all the soldiers, at least everyone seemed to be relieved that the screaming and shouting had run its course.

I was more shaken by that birthing experience than by any of the other medical emergencies I found myself dealing with. During the years I served in Vietnam I learned to deal with traumatic wounds without much fanfare, although amputating the arm of that Vietnamese paratrooper was the most serious example of medical care I attempted. Even in that case I understood what was required and I did the best I could. Nevertheless, as I knelt between that woman's knees on a dirty basement floor and pulled on that baby's head I knew I was in deep water. In fact, I learned more about women, labor, birth canals, and resilient babies than I had ever really wanted to know. That was a traumatic moment for me, and I can only assume the poor woman recovered from the whole experience faster than I did.

24
A Shattered Image

Enemy artillery impacting inside the An Loc perimeter remained at such a level of intensity that staying alive above ground was very chancy. The battalion's defensive lines had been adjusted so the troops could move into buildings providing some degree of protection. Fighting positions were selected that offered good visibility and grazing fire down streets and alleys, across intersections, and into nearby ruins occupied by the enemy. Most of the buildings in the inner part of the city were constructed of cement block or poured concrete, and when knocked apart the rubble could be stacked and piled to make protected fighting positions. Some of the structures had basements, and soldiers took turns going below ground to rest and cook when they weren't engaged in confronting the enemy.

In many cases North Vietnamese soldiers were directly across the street from our positions, and their proximity was emphasized when several paratroopers told me they had heard enemy leaders instructing their men to catch the American. As far as I knew I was the only American in the area and was surprised the North Vietnamese had seen me, or even knew I was close-by. There was very little comfort in learning the enemy would rather catch than kill me, and I spent a number of restless hours in the dead of night thinking through my limited options if capture should suddenly become imminent.

The rifle company's strong points and fighting positions stretched about four blocks. They were mutually supporting and tied in with other units on both flanks. Once the adjustments had been completed to Colonel Hieu's satisfaction, he decided to move the command group off the front line and into a more central location. Since there were only a half dozen of us, our needs were dictated more by security than size. The battalion commander detailed me to locate a more suitable place to move into. I took a pair of soldiers from upstairs to keep me company, and the three of us went scurrying through the destruction behind the forward positions in search of a good command post. Peering into a walled compound about halfway down the line and on the back side of the block, we found a one-story house with windows in the foundation, indicating a basement. It appeared a likely location and warranted a closer examination.

There wasn't any sign of life in the place as I ran through the back door and into the kitchen. Artillery fire had smashed holes in the roof, and the rooms were trashed and littered with broken tiles and rubbish. My two companions started going through the rooms to ensure they were clear. I saw the basement door and paused to listen for any sounds from below before I cautiously went down the steps. When I got to the bottom I poked my shotgun around a corner and glimpsed a threatening figure moving at the end of the dim hallway. My response was immediate—I triggered off a load of oo buckshot and quickly jerked back out of sight. The blast of the shotgun was followed by cement chips and pellets bouncing off the walls. I reached around the corner and pumped three more loads of buckshot down the hallway. There wasn't any return fire. I quickly reloaded my shotgun and knelt down to peer around the corner, but couldn't see anyone on the floor. Just dust and gunsmoke floating in the air. I was getting ready to roll a grenade down the hall when it all began to come into a better focus. The frame of a large mirror on the far wall was smashed and knocked cockeyed. The menacing presence I'd glimpsed had disappeared with the mirror.

That was a serious moment of self-recognition and reappraisal for me. First of all it came as something of a surprise to realize I had developed such a hair trigger in An Loc's environment of stress and survival. I had not even considered a non-hostile possibility before I shot. I was also sobered by how much my physical appearance had changed, and obviously not for the better. I certainly hadn't recognized the figure at the end of the hall.

Even though the battalion's soldiers stayed under cover day and night, gossip still traveled with amazing speed. Only a few of the officers ventured to joke with me about the mirror incident, but I'm sure every man in the battalion was much amused by the American's jumpy behavior. So while I didn't fully appreciate the funny side of it at the time, my paratrooper comrades must have enjoyed the recounting, particularly as they could easily see themselves and one another in the story. They probably also decided to resist any urge to wander out in front of the nervous American and his shotgun if at all possible.

25
Tanks in Town

The North Vietnamese ran armor into the city on a number of occasions following their first appearance on 13 April. They often appeared without the infantry support necessary for their protection, and when they were caught roaming unprotected in the confines of the city they were vulnerable.[1] Occasionally a single tank showed up wandering by itself; on other occasions two or three seemed to be operating together. Their behavior was unpredictable and erratic. Enemy armor didn't subscribe to any tactical doctrine familiar to me, and ignoring the fundamentals of combined arms operations worked against them every time.

While many tanks were killed on the approaches to the city, a number succeeded in getting into town to include areas controlled by the South Vietnamese defenders. When that happened they went roaring up and down streets, crashing through backyards, and generally spreading fear and trepidation among the troops. The South Vietnamese were not well equipped to take on tanks, and most of the enemy's armored vehicles were killed by American aircraft. Cobra helicopters and fast-moving fighters deserved much of the credit, but AC-130 gunships also made successful attacks when they could get a visual or pick up an engine's heat signature. However it happened, every time a tank was destroyed the defenders offered up a rousing shout of thanks and praise.

The M-72 Light Anti-tank Weapon, the LAW, was the only tank-killing weapon available to the soldiers of the battalion. That was the same one-shot shoulder-fired rocket launcher we'd previously used to attack enemy bunkers. When fired at an armored vehicle, however, the LAW had to be employed with squinty-eyed deliberation. Some of a tank's best protection, particularly the turret and front glacis, could defeat a LAW, and no one wanted to shoot without getting a kill for all the obvious reasons. The best way to destroy a tank was to get an airplane to do it. But in the absence of that remedy, the next best option was to let the vehicle go past and then shoot it in the rear with a LAW. Another alternative was to shoot down into a tank from an upper story, but that was chancy in the city's artillery-riddled environment. The best plan for the infantry soldier, if push came to shove and he had to suck it up, was to shoot one of the vehicle's more lightly protected parts, hopefully destroying the engine or possibly igniting fuel or ammunition.

It required a lot of sand for a man to take on a main battle tank when the only arrow in his quiver was a five-pound LAW; everyone knew there wouldn't be much time for follow-up shots if the initial whack didn't do the trick. During the course of the battle South Vietnamese soldiers did face that grim reality on a number of occasions and succeed in killing tanks with LAWs. While most of those kinds of mano y mano confrontations occurred before the battalion moved into town, I was present on one noteworthy occasion when paratroopers managed to kill a T-54 with LAWs. It was the kind of thing that could have gone bad fast, but it was also a very exciting and deeply satisfying experience—more about that later. On another adrenalin-pumping day I had a very personal encounter with a tank, a sweat-popping confrontation I found particularly stressful because I found myself alone in a face-off that was totally unexpected.

That particular incident was directly linked to Colonel Walter Ulmer, the senior advisor to the 5th ARVN Division and the highest-ranking American officer in the city. His place of business was in the division's headquarters bunker, across town from my location. Colonel Ulmer had assumed responsibility for setting priorities and allocating scarce resources necessary to fight the battle, and he managed tactical aircraft very carefully because they were so critical to the defense. It all made sense to me, as long as I wasn't ignored as had happened on 11 May when I was forced to wait in line for hours before getting that team of star-crossed Cobras. I had begun to suspect, from my limited perspective and perhaps a bit churlishly, that the system was being used to ensure headquarters security while the needs of the great unwashed out in the suburbs represented a lesser concern. I couldn't do anything about my concerns as long as the battalion was south of town in the rubber plantation, but after we moved into An Loc I was within better reach of the rule-maker, and that made me harder to ignore.

My blood pressure finally hit critical mass the day I requested an air strike on an active target a hundred yards outside the battalion's sector, and the answer was a resounding and unapologetic no. That turn-down was particularly galling, and possibly even ungrateful as the battalion had so recently cleaned out an especially dangerous enemy penetration in the garrison's pe-rimeter. After discussing the issue on the radio with my boss, Colonel Tay-lor, I talked to Colonel Ulmer directly, but to no avail. Colonel Hieu refused to get involved after my request had been denied. I suspected he didn't want to be seen as pleading for favors, but beyond that he wouldn't chance being embarrassed by some American refusing his personal request.

Colonel Hieu tried to dissuade me from pursuing the issue when I told him I intended to have a face-to-face discussion with the American colonel. Insisting that making the trip wasn't worth the danger from incoming fire, Colonel Hieu refused to send anyone with me. Even so I decided it was time to have a serious discussion with the senior American officer in town. I wasn't absolutely sure where his bunker was located, but if I wanted to have a per-sonal meeting I would have to find it since Colonel Ulmer wasn't going to come see me. I knew getting air support was an urgent issue that could not be ignored, so I grabbed my radio and shotgun and got ready to go find the man who controlled the air strikes.

The threat posed by incoming fire was a legitimate concern, demanding serious consideration. Since the tremendous artillery bombardments of late April, the number of enemy shells impacting in the friendly perimeter had decreased to a daily rate of 1,000 to 2,500 rounds of all types to include ar-tillery, mortar, and tank main gun rounds.[2] For the soldiers in the town, the term "friendly perimeter" had long since become a cruel oxymoron. To get some perspective on what those numbers meant for people living inside the bull's eye, it's instructive to compare the agony of An Loc with two better-known Vietnam battles where artillery played an important role.

The epic struggle for Dien Bien Phu took place from March to May 1954, and as that battle developed the number of rounds impacting the French po-sitions grew to approximately 2,000 a day.[3] The French had counted on air support to ensure the viability of their defense, and the garrison was doomed when its aerial supply and tactical air requirements could not be met.

In another noteworthy case a daily average of 150 shells slammed into the main defensive positions during the battle of Khe Sanh, fought from January to April 1968. Thirteen hundred and seven rounds impacted on 23 February, the most intense day of that battle.[4] The worst day for incoming rounds at Khe Sanh matched the daily average smashing into An Loc for more than three months. Much like the An Loc garrison, the troops defending Khe Sanh received massive support from the air. Unlike An Loc, however, accounts of the Khe Sanh battle also received an ocean of ink and eventually became en-shrined as a singular feat of American arms. While the defenders of Dien Bien Phu and Khe Sanh were certainly subjected to serious bombardments, in neither case did their experience approach the estimated 78,000 rounds fired into An Loc during the course of that appalling battle.[5]

The incessant shelling was mind numbing, although the arrival of individual rounds seemed arbitrary and unpredictable. Throughout the course of the battle shattering explosions continued to knock down walls and churn up trash and maim and kill men who had taken every precaution to escape the danger. Some kind of protection was absolutely essential for survival as those rounds arrived in an area little more than twelve blocks square. The distance I intended to travel was probably seven or eight blocks, but it was hard to judge because of conditions in the city. At that point the place was mostly piles of rubble, strewn with every kind of rubbish and filth, all being further plowed up and pulverized by the incessant fire as the town cooked in the blistering heat.

There were other dangers to face when traveling in the city that included small-arms fire both aimed and capricious. We were also told friendly troops had planted land mines early in the battle when it seemed the whole city might be overrun. No one knew where those mines were located, but I assumed they were in the dirt of backyards and ditches, intended to force the enemy out into the defender's fields of fire.

I must have told Colonel Ulmer I was coming to visit because I expected to find him in the South Vietnamese commanding general's bunker. So off I went down a back street in the direction of my quest. It was midafternoon and I was in a hurry because I wanted to get the issue settled before another night arrived. After running fifty yards or so I hunkered down in a concrete gutter to get below the level of the street. It took a couple of minutes to catch my breath while I looked around, then it was time to struggle on. I was reclining in another ditch farther down the street, peering toward the enemy part of town, when I thought I saw a building begin to shift and bulge. The structure was a couple of blocks away, and I blinked hard to clear my focus, but it still seemed to be moving.

Then part of the wall fell out and a tank began to appear, and suddenly it clanked out into the street in a cloud of dust and diesel exhaust. I could hear the squeal of drive sprockets and the crunch of steel treads on broken concrete. The torn-up fenders, sloppy tracks, and low silhouette of a T-54 were clearly visible. An enemy tank suddenly revealing itself was an unexpected and unwelcome surprise, and I scrunched lower in the ditch to watch the monstrous thing. I stared in disbelief as the turret swung around and the main gun came to rest aimed right down my street, seemingly directly at me. I wiggled deeper into the filth hoping a mine wouldn't explode just as a 100 mm cannon shell blasted past me about head high. I was frozen in place.

Then it fired again and another giant shell went tearing down the street after the first one. My shotgun was badly overmatched and I was in a pickle.

I didn't know what he was shooting at, probably just firing blindly into the friendly part of town. For a moment I thought he might actually be shooting at me, but that seemed preposterous. I was sure he couldn't see me down in the ditch, but lying there long enough for him to come down the street and find me didn't seem like a good idea either. Jumping up and running was an equally bad option because I knew there was a coaxial machine gun mounted in the turret pointing wherever the main gun was aimed, and at that moment it was looking in my direction. The whole event probably didn't last more than a minute or two, and it came to an end when the tank suddenly reversed back into the building in a cloud of dust. The roof on the building seemed to settle as he disappeared from view. I quickly scurried on down the street and within minutes was in the 5th ARVN Division's headquarters bunker, standing toe-to-toe with the garrison's senior American officer.

Our meeting got off to a rocky start, particularly once the depth and relative comfort and safety of Colonel Ulmer's abode became more evident. Still shaking from my recent fright, I found myself becoming thoroughly angry as I compared the safety of his bunker with the conditions under which I was laboring. I was outraged and he seemed preoccupied and our conversation very quickly became an unseemly shouting match between a captain and a colonel. There were a number of other people standing around in the gloom to include members of his advisory team, but not one of them was invited or felt inclined to join the discussion. I did notice the Vietnamese division commander, Brigadier General Le Van Hung, off to the side. General Hung had an embarrassed grin on his face as he observed the Americans participating in a candid and free-flowing exchange of views that would never have been tolerated in his army.

Much to Colonel Ulmer's credit, he reined in his ire and let me have my say. Then it was his turn and he explained the air support priorities he was using for the defense of the city. Although he provided an insightful brief on managing scarce resources at the division level, I refused to be placated until the 5th Airborne Battalion's requirements had been fully explored. Our conversation lasted less than five minutes and I was ready to leave when Colonel Ulmer agreed the battalion's area of responsibility might qualify for some of the air support. As I picked up my gear I told him the first strike I was going to request would be on a tank just down the street from where he was living. He thought that would be a grand idea.

I saluted as Colonel Ulmer returned to his maps. Incoming shells were exploding outside the bunker's entrance so I waited a few minutes before

15. & 16. Rust on the tanks, T-54 (above), and PT-76 (below), indicates that Lieutenant Colonel Greg Wilcox took these photos some time after the fight was over. Courtesy of Carruthers, *The Battle of An Loc: A Massive Convergence of Forces.*

17. & 18. North Vietnamese armored vehicles destroyed during the battle. Photos courtesy of Pham, vnafmamn.

climbing the concrete steps. After pausing at the top for another moment to double-check, I began the process of moving to where I could get a look at the building hiding the tank. Once I was sure I had the right location I contacted the FAC, who marked the target for a pair of orbiting jets. The tank crew should have gotten the message when the rocket went off, but perhaps they were enjoying a last siesta because they made no effort to escape the incoming attack. The first bomb hit right next to the building with a tremendous explosion and threw pieces of assorted junk all around the neighborhood. The second jet was right behind his buddy and right on target. The building was wrecked and the tank began to burn. I could see its main gun drooping in the fire as a thick column of oily smoke climbed slowly into a clear blue sky.

After thanking the FAC and asking him to pass on a hearty well done to the fighter pilots, I continued to make my weary way back to my basement. I had been surprised and sobered by my poor physical condition during the cross-town trip, and the journey back seemed even more laborious. I felt exhausted, shuffling from ditch to ditch, sweating, and mumbling curses. That was the last time I recall talking to the senior American officer in the city. We didn't have much to discuss once the battalion started getting the air support necessary to better hold up our end of the deal.

The tank destroyed that afternoon was outside our lines and I never got a close look at it. But before leaving An Loc I did inspect several others that showed a lot of wear and tear. Filthy and stinking, they had become another symbol of the enemy's failure to take the city.

26

The Enemy's Worst Nightmare
Was Named Spectre

During the course of the war the U.S. Air Force introduced a series of large, fixed-wing, multiengine gunships that provided close and accurate fire support to troops on the ground.[1] From the perspective of the soldier those big gunships were a life-saving weapon that could be depended on to deliver a tremendous volume of fire when and where most needed. With each new generation of gunships came improved communications systems, day and night targeting systems, weapons systems, and computer technology to pull it all together. One of the features common to all those aircraft was how their weapons systems fired out the left side. That allowed the pilots to circle and keep an eye on the target while the crew cranked out the rounds.

Each version shared several other common features that made them particularly valuable to troops calling for their assistance. They all carried a great deal of fuel so they could loiter over the battlefield for hours. They carried a big load of flares and could illuminate very effectively for long periods of time. Their size also allowed them to bring a lot of ammunition to the fight. Of great importance, gunships were also equipped with FM radios so troops on the ground could talk directly to the air crews, minimizing potential confusion or misunderstandings. The devastating volume and pinpoint accuracy of the fire those aircraft delivered, plus their responsiveness, often spelled the difference between life and death for soldiers. Just the sound of those big engines droning high overhead could have an admonitory effect on the enemy, particularly when they came to realize the gunships could find and kill them day or night.

The U.S. Air Force gunships I called on to provide close fire support during my first tour in Vietnam were converted twin-engine C-47 transports using the call sign Spooky. The troops also knew Spooky, now an AC-47, as Puff the Magic Dragon because of the ripping roar and fiery display the aircraft's three 7.62 miniguns made when they were turned on. Updated gatling guns, their spinning barrels hosed down the target area at a rate of 6,000 rounds a minute per gun. Puff was particularly impressive after dark when the torrents of red tracers seemed to sweep out of the night sky and scour the earth like a monster's breath. Puff the Magic Dragon was a very popular and reassuring friend when most needed.[2]

That aircraft was replaced by Shadow, a modification of the venerable old twin engine/twin tail Flying Boxcar. In addition to a lot of loiter time and a big load of ammunition and flares, the redesignated AC-119 Shadow also carried a giant spotlight and a night observation sight that allowed the crew to more accurately engage targets after dark. When cornered by Shadow, the enemy found the aircraft's four 7.62 miniguns a lethal experience. Another version of the AC-119 gunship called Stinger was equipped with a pair of 20 mm multi-barrel gatling-type cannons as well as four 7.62 miniguns. Stinger was built primarily to kill truck convoys on the Ho Chi Minh trail, but Shadow and Stinger were both important steps toward the development of the big brother of them all, the truly magnificent four-engine AC-130 Spectre.[3]

That newer and much more lethal gunship had been deployed prior to my service with the Vietnamese Airborne. The version of Spectre in use at that time was the prototype of the space-age AC-130 found in the arsenal today. But even that first model provided a quantum improvement in everything ground troops wanted and needed from a big gunship. The jump in capability included Spectre's armament, which was truly awe inspiring. The aircraft carried a pair of 20 mm Vulcan cannons, a Bofors 40 mm cannon, and a 105 mm howitzer. The crew often used the 40 mm cannon to zero in on a target and then they would follow up with rounds from the 105 mm howitzer. That gun was in its own special category of aerial fire support, providing a precise and deadly hammer that made a serious statement on the battlefield. Spectre also came equipped with a low-light television camera plus other equipment that amplified ambient light very effectively. Those various capabilities were all tied into a computerized fire control system maximizing on-target effectiveness. Spectre's hi-tech systems resulted in a much-improved ability to find and attack the enemy after dark. Troops felt blessed when Spectre answered the phone, and the soldiers in An Loc made a lot of urgent calls.

The first time I used Spectre while serving with the 5th Airborne Battalion was the night before 51 Company accomplished its fatal Detachment-Left-In-Contact mission. At that time we were bracing for a major attack and I was getting all my fire support assets coordinated. After several small firefights flared out in the rubber trees, Colonel Hieu felt he had all the warning of the enemy's presence he needed and ordered our outposts back into the battalion perimeter. Soon after nightfall a Spectre came on station and I asked the air crew to use their sensors to look for heat sources in a big arc out to our front. I wanted to find the North Vietnamese in their assembly areas or while they were moving into their attack positions. Spectre was also responding to 6th Airborne Battalion requests that evening, but the gunship did a sweep of the area I'd requested without any positive hits.

I was disappointed there weren't any obvious targets for Spectre's big gun, but I did direct a fire mission on a possible troop concentration about a half mile east of my position. The gunship tore up the target area with 20 mm cannon fire. Once both the air crew and I were absolutely sure where the rounds were hitting, I adjusted the fire in closer and finally called a halt when rounds were chewing up the rubber trees about a hundred yards outside the battalion's trenches. That was close enough at that point, and it helped the air crew get a good fix on my location.

Spectre's capabilities made it the most effective weapon system for providing close air support after dark, and that's when the aircraft was normally on station. Therefore Spectre was not available as the enemy pushed into the battalion's position the following day. Even if an AC-130 had been there to participate in our defense I don't think its presence would have changed the outcome. To employ Spectre's weapons required holding off other ground attack aircraft while the big gunship fired. That kind of coordination always ate up valuable on-station time for either Spectre or the fighters. Considering the urgency of the requirement and the number of fast movers that were stacked up waiting their turn to enter the fight, the FAC and I had all we could do without further complicating an already demanding situation.

My best example of Spectre's versatility occurred after the battalion entered the city. The gunship demonstrated all its capabilities and impressed friend and foe alike the night we conducted that hasty attack to recapture lost ground. Our two rifle companies had succeeded in fighting their way through several blocks of destruction and rubble before the battalion commander ordered them to pause while supplies were brought forward. As they prepared to continue the attack I coordinated supporting fires with the FAC. Once the companies were ready they advanced into areas I had just hit with several air strikes, and then our right flank unit ran into stiff resistance from enemy fortified in a large L-shaped building. The troops had encountered a blizzard of small-arms fire from the building, and the company commander called for support. Spectre was on station and I knew it could generate an excellent solution for that particular problem. I instructed the company com-

19. An AC-130 Spectre in action over Vietnam. Note the aircraft is in a left-hand turn, allowing all weapons systems to bear on the target area. Photo courtesy of the U.S. Air Force.

mander to pull his men back and get behind good cover because Spectre would soon be firing.

The L-shaped building was indicated on my map by a symbol, so using grid coordinates I was able to locate it accurately. The Spectre crew was not absolutely sure they could identify that specific building from their maps, so I directed them to a road that came into the city farther to the northeast and had them follow it into town to a traffic round-about located several blocks north of the target. I instructed them to hit the round-about with their 40 mm cannon to ensure we were all referencing the same location on the ground. Once that happened I asked them to walk cannon fire toward me, down the street to the L-shaped building. As soon as the company commander verified that cannon fire was hitting the building we all knew we were ready for some serious fireworks.

I then instructed the Spectre crew to shoot the building with ten high-explosive 105 mm shells, starting from the end closest to the street and working the rounds through the building. I made sure the air crew understood that the paratroopers would assault when the tenth shell hit, so they had to limit their fire and count those shells carefully. Then I told the company commander to keep track of the shells as they hit and have his men take the building when the tenth round exploded. I figured ten high-explosive rounds walking through the building would kill some of the enemy and chase out the rest.

Spectre nailed the end of the building with several more 40 mm rounds to double-check and then began to fire the 105 mm cannon. The first shell hit with a terrific blast and a shower of fiery sparks, and it was followed by nine more smashing through the structure. Some enemy troops did try to get out the back door only to run into a machine-gun ambush that had been quickly established by a squad of paratroopers. The shrapnel from the tenth round was still whining through the air when the paratroopers were on their feet and moving. They shot their way inside to find very little resistance. About twenty dead or dying North Vietnamese were in the shattered rooms, and the ambush outside the back door killed another half dozen. It was three o'clock in the morning when the attack started. The whole event lasted about twenty minutes and went off like clockwork.

Spectre's supporting fires filled the bill and there were no friendly casualties in that action. The paratroopers were able to continue forward and quickly closed on the cross street marking their limit of advance. Ever vigilant and always responsive, Spectre was our tireless nighttime friend—and certainly the enemy's worst nightmare.

27
Disjointed Events

Unremitting day-and-night shelling plus filthy and debilitating living conditions, bad to begin with and progressively worse over time, became the most influential aspects of my existence. Those were the core realities setting the tone for life during the battle, and I slowly began to accept an extraordinarily bizarre circumstance as somehow becoming near normal. More a comment on bending to life-as-it-exists than anything else, I found myself in a lethal and unwholesome environment that could not be escaped. Neither could it be ameliorated other than through adapting where possible and ignoring the rest. It was an exercise in adjusting various pain thresholds.

When the battalion moved out of the rubber plantation and into town we gained direct access to airdropped supplies and were able to get all the small-arms ammunition, LAWs, and grenades we could use. The quality of our food also improved. While I couldn't rebuild my physical condition on C-rations, packed with calories though they may have been, the raging diarrhea of previous weeks seemed to moderate. Wounded soldiers received very little professional care although some medical supplies were included in the pallets being parachuted in. A garrison medical holding area had been organized close to the soccer field but only the most basic treatments were available. When helicopters stopped flying into town there was no compelling reason to move our injured there. Hard-hit soldiers were carried to the battalion aid station, and the number of wounded continued to increase until roughly half the men shouldering weapons were bandaged. Those with bad injuries were in big trouble. Our newest cemetery began to grow.

The number of uninjured soldiers was growing smaller, causing levels of stress to increase. Those men seemed to share a growing fatalism as their comrades were felled by small-arms fire, shrapnel from random shelling, and other forms of bad luck. An Loc was an unhealthy place in every respect and the psychological stresses served to underscore the physical dangers and discomforts. Considering the length of time the men were engaged in that do-or-die fight, I marveled at how well they held up.

I recall only the one soldier in the bomb crater who was so traumatized he couldn't function although there may have been others who were protected and cared for by their buddies. I'm sure, however, that every man in the battalion was psychologically wounded to some extent as a result of the intensity and duration of the battle. The majority were already seasoned veterans when they were trucked out of Saigon, but none had undergone anything like the rigors of the An Loc fight.

The intensity of that experience certainly added to any mental burdens they might have brought with them. As a veteran I know a cumulative effect builds from prolonged exposure to the hazards of combat. I'd arrived at Team 162 enjoying a certain degree of hyper-alertness so living with soldiers who compulsively cleaned their weapons, ducked at the least provocation, and slept fitfully was very familiar to me. In fact I found all those battlefield behaviors reassuring, knowing my companions could be trusted to be keeping watch, ready for the enemy. That was the accepted, even the expected norm in that kind of outfit, in that kind of place. I understood those soldiers and their twitchy ways because I was a charter member of the club.

When my two-man advisor team was reduced to one I initially tried viewing my new situation as a wonderfully unique and challenging enterprise. I could visualize the eventual grandkids mesmerized as I recounted my adventures as the only American in a Vietnamese paratrooper battalion. In fact the experience quickly began to wear thin. I knew Colonel Taylor couldn't do anything about my solo act and the battalion commander wasn't concerned as long as the link to American support was working.

Early on Colonel Hieu had defined my role in the battalion, and he cast me as a useful functionary who could be ignored until American firepower was needed. I didn't speak Vietnamese but that wasn't the issue. Colonel Hieu spoke good English and could have included me in discussions or otherwise shared information but chose not to. I resented his studied indifference on several levels, but at the least I thought the critical nature of my contribution to the battalion's success warranted a greater degree of inclusion than it got.

While I was confident I could handle the job by myself, it would have been a much more positive undertaking to team with another American of any rank or background. Standing shifts and getting the sleep required to be sharp when it really counted would have provided an immediate benefit.

Having an alter ego who possessed a shared cultural background that offered points of commonality not always possible with my Vietnamese comrades would also have been healthy.

But I didn't have that person to commiserate with, to share the day-to-day kinds of events that made up life in the trenches. Exchanging reminiscences and aspirations or providing psychological support to balance out mood swings is a team activity. Even though there were Americans within a half mile, they might just as well have been on the other side of the planet. I was on my own and a growing feeling of isolation became more compelling with the passing weeks. I began to wonder, if I should be killed would I be shoveled into the ground by myself? Or would I get buried together with some of the battalion's dead? While those arrangements probably wouldn't matter a great deal, I also wondered if anyone besides my folks would know or care, or ever find out where I was.

A more clear-cut symptom of my mental condition began to reappear, a very specific point of pressure and coldness that developed on the back of my head. The spot was just behind my right ear and became more and more sensitive and compelling with time. It actually became painful. That feeling was a return of the same sensation I'd experienced during an earlier tour.

The previous feeling had faded when I was away from Vietnam but it began to remanifest during the fighting in the rubber plantation on the south side of town. With time that point of pressure on my skull became more insistent. It was the exact spot where I was going to be shot or hit by shrapnel, and I knew it. When it first began to reappear I worried about it and wore my helmet tipped back and stood against trees or walls to protect the spot. Eventually I simply waited to get smacked in the back of the head. Although I knew full well that I was experiencing a traumatic reaction to the danger and stress of the environment I could not will it to stop and I could not ignore it either.

As the battle developed and casualties mounted I waited to get hit. With time it was simply inevitable. The difference between myself and the others was that I knew exactly how I would be killed, and I was constantly reminded by the painfully pressing spot. I eventually left An Loc with nothing more serious than a tendency to twitch and a pair of ringing ears and was delighted that all my body parts were intact. It took months for the painful spot on the back of my skull to fade away again.

Despite those concerns, there were times when I convinced myself I had to stretch my legs. Sometimes I decided to check on something or other, but often I simply wanted to escape the endless tedium and physical inactivity of my confining circumstance. And tedious it was. I hadn't received any mail after the air assault and had also neglected to bring anything to read. A thick collection of something to ponder would have been most welcome. The already scant menu of discussion topics I could share with Colonel Hieu was further limited by my lack of enthusiasm for exploring the many failings of western civilization and American culture. I deeply regretted the death of the battalion surgeon for several reasons, not least because he was an intelligent and interesting man whose conversation was stimulating and amusing. But he was gone, another reason for me to look outside the narrow preoccupations of the command group.

The tenor of the battle began to change after the battalion moved into town. Dangers posed by incoming artillery remained persistent but enemy infantry started pulling in their horns. They seemed to be losing the initiative and instead of persistently attacking they dug in and stubbornly defended. Their new behavior encouraged an assertive response from some of the South Vietnamese and small groups of paratroopers occasionally went hunting. Turning the tables on the enemy seemed a constructive way to vent some of the frustration and anger, and I joined the hunters on several occasions. Those moments have retained a distinct and compelling vividness.

On one occasion I remember lying on a pulverized sidewalk in the midday sun. The temperature was in the 90s and dust was rising off the cement in the heat waves. Sweat was running down my face and under my filthy uniform. I was with a half dozen paratroopers as we listened to North Vietnamese voices inside the building we were hugging. The enemy didn't realize we were there, right outside and under a row of empty windows. Using hand signals and pantomime I made sure each of the paratroopers had a fragmentation grenade, and when everyone was ready we pulled the pins and tossed the grenades inside. The blasts came as a surprise to the occupants, and when the troops followed the grenades through the windows there was a lot of chasing around through various rooms.

The troops zeroed in on the moaning and groaning and once the building was cleared we took a break. There were about a dozen North Vietnamese inside, dead in their pith helmets and khaki uniforms. Most were armed with AK-47 assault rifles although several had been carrying rocket-propelled grenade launchers. The dust and dirt in the stifling rooms had been stirred up and mixed with cordite from the grenades and gunfire. Fresh blood was splattered against the walls and puddling on the floors. One paratrooper had been shot through the foot, but no one else was injured. Grateful to be out of the sun and out of sight, we hunkered down so we wouldn't be exposed to incoming fire and stayed alert to preclude a rude surprise.

On another occasion, possibly the same day or maybe not, I recall lying in an alley, pressed up against the foundation of a building with a group of paratroopers. We could hear North Vietnamese talking inside and I signaled the troops to get ready. I got up on my knees and lifted my shotgun over my head and emptied it through a window. All five rounds of oo buckshot got pumped inside the place. Pellets were still zinging around when the paratroopers charged in and focused on the shouting my shotgun had produced. I didn't follow until I had reloaded from the claymore bag of shells I was carrying, but I reloaded fast because I didn't like being left alone.

I ventured out of the basement command post on another occasion to go looking for a tank that was reported on the loose. Unlike my previous tank experience, this was an effort launched with malicious intent. About ten of us worked our way around the neighborhood for an hour or so without finding anything, then we moved into the wreck of a commercial building. I took half the soldiers and crawled onto the second floor to get a view of the area and the other men stayed downstairs to protect our backs. Normally no one would venture into such an exposed position and we weren't going to push our luck by staying very long. Careful to remain down on the floor and away from the windows, we scanned the neighborhood.

There were two big rooms on the second level, littered with smashed office furniture and assorted rubbish. The floors were covered with files and papers, broken roof tiles, shards of glass, and pieces of cement block. There wasn't much roof and plenty of holes in the walls so we could look around without being too obvious. We were getting ready to leave when the squad downstairs radioed they had glimpsed the thing moving about a block away. It was coming down the alley behind the building and taking its time so we had a few minutes to get set.

The men were carrying half a dozen LAWs, which were quickly armed. Two soldiers who had shot the weapon before became the designated gunners. There wasn't a very good angle to shoot into the alley so we decided to sit tight until the tank would be more visible from our front windows. We could hear the thing before we could see it, and when the long main gun finally poked around the corner of the building we waited for our target to follow.

We couldn't see any infantry moving with it. The engine was roaring and belching diesel smoke and steel treads were scrabbling and squealing in the rubble-strewn street as it maneuvered under our windows. Once it began to move away the two LAW gunners leaned out and fired their missiles. They were aiming down and into the top of the monstrous thing, hopefully at the back deck and the engine compartment. As soon as they fired they both reached back for more LAWs and shot all we had in quick time.

20. South Vietnamese soldiers getting ready to engage T-54 tanks with M-72 LAWs during the battle. Photo courtesy of Pham, vnafmamn.

I'm not sure how many of the rockets actually hit because the beast continued to grind along for a few yards before it lurched to a stop, but then it went ballistic. The back deck was on fire and then the turret hatch flew open and crewmen started scrambling out. The troops were ready and none of the North Vietnamese made it to the ground alive. Ammunition began to cook off as we charged down the stairs. Dramatic fireworks quickly developed out in the street and oily smoke was soon boiling above the rooftops, marking the demise of another T-54.

By some estimates there were more than 20,000 civilians living in An Loc when the Easter Offensive began to unfold. That number undoubtedly increased as refugees from outlying areas fled the first phase of the North Vietnamese invasion. Once the enemy closed in on the city a flood of people moved farther south to escape the fighting, although many thousands remained behind. Getting away became virtually impossible after Highway 13 became a battleground although I heard some were able to leave by hiking cross country. Just finding the basic necessities was a life-and-death struggle for the remaining civilians as the fight for the city became more intense.

Like the soldiers, civilians burrowed into the basements to escape small-arms fire and the massive artillery attacks. There were no humanitarian support systems available. The neighborhood clinics and the hospitals were abandoned and destroyed along with the rest of the city's infrastructure. The living cared for their wounded and buried their dead. There may well have been

21. A destroyed T-54 in An Loc. Photo courtesy of Pham, vnafmamn.

several thousand civilians living underground in the city as the battle wore down, but except for my experience with the new mother and her group in that basement, they remained largely invisible to me.

I did see a crowd out in the open in one instance, and their audacity quickly turned into a brutal catastrophe. That event occurred when the battalion was still in the rubber plantation on the south side of town. One morning, without any prior indication, a large gaggle of civilians began walking down Highway 13 and out of the battle. They had come together someplace in the city and evidently felt that attempting to walk out was better than staying. There were at least a hundred people in the throng to include men, women, and children. Many were carrying suitcases and bundles, others were waving white flags. They knew the North Vietnamese controlled the road but had decided to throw themselves on the mercy of the enemy in hopes of being allowed to leave. It was not to be.

The group had gone less than a half mile past our positions when the North Vietnamese opened fire with a barrage of mortar shells. A number of people were immediately wounded while others were killed and a stampede started back toward town. The survivors carried their wounded as they struggled up the road but the luggage was abandoned and the dead lay where they fell.

Much later I learned that during the first days of the battle the North Vietnamese had fired on a crowd of refugees in a church. Based on the highway incident I witnessed there was no question the enemy deliberately targeted and terrorized civilians. I could think of several reasons for their savagery. They undoubtedly wanted to stress the An Loc garrison by forcing civilians to stay while also demonstrating the South Vietnamese government's inability to protect their own people. But whatever their purpose, the North Vietnamese inflicted an unnecessary brutality by killing hundreds and traumatizing thousands of innocents who were caught up in the fighting.

There were times when I was worried about being captured. Never for a moment did I ever doubt the bravery or the loyalty of the soldiers I was serving with, or the cohesiveness of the unit. Being left behind or somehow abandoned never crossed my mind. What I did think about was the possibility of the battalion being overrun and then getting captured. Several times when we were defending the southern approaches to the town ground attacks were so heavy the enemy got into our position before being killed, and we had no place to go. During those attacks dozens of North Vietnamese died in the wire and farther out in the rubber trees trying to get up to our position. There were hundreds of the enemy involved and during those times I thought through several of my options should the battalion be overwhelmed.

My first choice was to grab some paratroopers and make a fighting withdrawal across the road to join our brothers in the 8th Airborne Battalion. If that wasn't possible, we might be able to cross the open ground to the friendly troops in the southern portion of the city. Those courses of action made some sense because we would be able to link with other defenders and continue providing some cohesion to the garrison's perimeter.

Option two was to gather a group of soldiers and move southeast away from the city and into the rubber plantations. That would follow the general direction of egress the survivors of the 6th Airborne Battalion had taken when they evacuated their hilltop fire base. Any effort to escape demanded that we stay well away from Highway 13 where major concentrations of North Vietnamese were located. Much would depend on stamina and good luck as it would be a long hike out with or without an eventual helicopter extraction.

The only other option was to climb a rubber tree and hope to go undetected. However much the thought of trying to monkey up fifteen feet of slick rubber tree trunk in a firefight might have amused me at the time, I couldn't have taken it very seriously. But under any circumstance, the idea of trying to surrender to the enemy in the turmoil of being overrun was not an option and didn't bear serious consideration. If I'd actually been pushed into a corner with no choices I'd have shot it out, hoping for the best and accepting the worst.

I stopped worrying about being captured after we moved into the city even though that was where the troops overheard North Vietnamese discussing their nefarious plans for me. Despite the enemy's close proximity, not to mention their evil intentions, it seemed much less likely they would be able to overrun and destroy the battalion at that point. Even though we were about half the strength we had been when we made the airmobile assault, the surviving paratroopers were extraordinarily tough and tenacious. I was confident they would fight to the last man; there was no doubt I was in good company in that regard.

No other South Vietnamese units were able to augment the An Loc garrison after the 1st Airborne Brigade and the 81st Airborne Ranger Group joined the fight. Helicopters had delivered some soldiers before that traffic was curtailed. Parachuting troops into town wasn't feasible given the small size of the drop zone and the lethality of antiaircraft fire throughout the area. But even without reinforcements the infantry battle in the city eventually stabilized. Perhaps the better description is that it slowly degenerated into a gunfight between exhausted soldiers struggling for survival in a moonscape of smashed buildings and abandoned spaces.

Meanwhile, the battle to reopen Highway 13 continued to grind along although no one in the 5th Airborne Battalion had a clear idea of its progress. We had been told there were positive developments although we didn't know anything specific. I was aware my tour was about up, but I didn't spend much time thinking about leaving when there wasn't any real indication of an end to the battle. Although I had lost track of the dates I clearly remember the afternoon I got a call from the brigade senior advisor, Colonel Taylor, telling me to pack up my gear and move to his location. He didn't give me a reason, but I knew a helicopter pad was close to his bunker and that was enough for me to consider happy possibilities.

When I told Colonel Hieu I had been ordered to move he simply turned away without a comment, a handshake, or a salute. Our relationship had never been positive and the fact I was leaving without a replacement on hand didn't improve his attitude. He hadn't appreciated getting a captain rather than a major to begin with. Over time I had learned how sensitive he was about the South Vietnamese army's inability to defeat the Easter Offensive without massive American support. Colonel Hieu was resentful of my presence, angered by my departure, upset that I wasn't being replaced, and didn't try to hide his conflicted feelings. The battalion operations officer made a point of shaking hands as I packed my rucksack, but it didn't take long to shoulder my gear and depart the filthy basement.

The trip to Colonel Taylor's bunker took some time, but I eventually arrived without incident after examining a burned-out tank sitting no more

22. Photo of downtown An Loc by Lieutenant Alan Tigner, courtesy of Carruthers, *The Battle of An Loc: A Massive Convergence of Forces.*

23. Another view of the city, photo courtesy of Lieutenant Bill Carruthers.

than twenty yards from the bunker entrance. Once down the steps and in-side I was welcomed with handshakes all around, and Colonel Taylor made a point of introducing me to the soldiers who had killed the tank. He also told me units moving up from the south were making progress and the 1st Airborne Brigade would return to Saigon as soon as the road was reopened. He mentioned that Colonel Hieu was being given the same news through his chain of command.

Colonel Taylor said my tour was up, and my orders to return to the United States were waiting on the personnel clerk's desk in Saigon. He then con-firmed that an American helicopter was going to try to get into the nearby pad the next morning. I and several others would go out if it appeared. It was time to go. I found a quiet spot in a far corner and dropped my gear on the floor with a profound sigh of relief.

Several soldiers were sharing a culinary adventure as they jockeyed to whip up something imaginative, mostly from C-ration ingredients liberally laced with hot sauce. It seemed the deep and commodious brigade bunker offered a social environment as well as a more varied diet than the spartan circum-stances I'd been surviving in. Even so, no one was able to conjure up the li-bations necessary to add some interest to the iodine-laced C-ration coffee.

28

The Ambivalence of Leaving

On one level I was overjoyed with the prospect of escaping the An Loc cesspool. The place was a filthy death trap and given my station in life I couldn't count on staying barricaded in a hole as deep and secure as a brigade or division bunker. I'd used up all the luck any one person could reasonably hope for and was fully aware I'd eventually get clipped if I persisted on rolling the dice. At the same time I was extraordinarily proud of the paratroopers of the 5th Airborne Battalion, and I valued my experience with those warriors more than I can say.

My service with the battalion had been an eye-opener on several levels. Vietnamese paratroopers had a routine casualty rate, and an attitude toward taking casualties, that I had not seen during my previous three years in Vietnam. Although American paratroopers were certainly not shy and took heavy casualties at times, the intensity of my experience with the Vietnamese Airborne was simply on a different scale. Vietnamese paratroopers were aggressive beyond belief at every level from squad to brigade. Assaults were ordered with little or no fire support, albeit often by necessity, and soldiers and officers routinely attacked with very little consideration for the personal costs involved. They expected and took casualties every time out of the blocks.

Unlike their American allies, Vietnamese paratroopers were irrevocably embroiled in an endless war. In my judgment that somber reality had a direct influence on the chain-of-command decision-making process as well as both individual and group behavior. The inherent aggressiveness of those soldiers meshed with a certain learned fatalism to produce the most lethal and violent combativeness once the shooting started. They attacked upright with single-minded focus; they simply concentrated on killing the enemy while ignoring danger. It seemed to me that most Vietnamese paratroopers did not expect to survive the war. They understood about dying and were not afraid of it.

Some kind of eventual retirement based on years of service was simply not relevant for the soldiers and officers of the Vietnamese Airborne Division.

As an example of resultant outcomes I offer my experience with the 5th Airborne Battalion. When we departed from Saigon on 8 April the battalion numbered approximately five hundred soldiers and thirty officers. Figuring in our replacements during the Highway 13 portion of the battle, roughly half the number of soldiers who had climbed into the trucks were dead and more than the remainder of that number had been wounded by the time the battalion returned to the capital. Some years later I read that the 1st Airborne Brigade's casualties totaled 1,425.[1] Using that number, and I suspect it's a low-ball figure considering what happened to the artillery battery and the 6th Airborne Battalion on their hilltop firebase, the overall casualty rate for the brigade approached 90 percent.

At any rate the link-up between South Vietnamese units coming up Highway 13 and the An Loc garrison finally occurred on 8 June. That happy event took place when paratroopers of the reconstituted 6th Airborne Battalion joined hands with their 8th Airborne Battalion brothers on the southern outskirts of the city. The next ARVN unit to arrive took over the 5th Airborne Battalion's portion of the perimeter. Several days later those three depleted airborne battalions pushed south out of town and fought another series of bloody engagements to destroy pockets of die-hard North Vietnamese still threatening Highway 13. Helicopters then picked up the brigade and flew it the next leg south to meet a convoy of trucks for the trip back to Saigon.

The three battalions accomplished a brief period of rebuilding before they were flown north to the province capital of Quang Tri. That city had been the first objective of the Easter Offensive and was still partially occupied by the enemy. Casualties were again heavy including 5th Airborne Battalion soldiers who were lost when a South Vietnamese aircraft accidentally bombed the unit. Based on my experience it seemed possible those pilots might have received inadequate targeting instructions. At any rate the misdirected attack dealt a devastating blow, and I was very sorry to hear about it.

Only recently have I been able to piece together a better understanding of the size of the forces involved in the fight for An Loc and the approximate human costs. At the height of the battle some 36,000 North Vietnamese were tasked with overrunning the city while another 10,000 were deployed south along Highway 13 to ensure overland communications were cut. Estimates of total enemy casualties run as high as 25,000 killed and wounded although the communists have never published reliable numbers.[2] One source states that approximately 80 of the enemy's tanks were destroyed during the An

24. 229th Assault Helicopter Battalion UH-1H slicks unloading troops on Highway 13 south of An Loc after link-up with the garrison had been accomplished. This was the only U.S. Army aviation unit awarded the Presidential Unit Citation twice during the Vietnam War.

25. Highway 13 being used as a landing zone to deliver troops to An Loc. Photos by Lieutenant Alan Tigner, courtesy of Carruthers, *The Battle of An Loc: A Massive Convergence of Forces.*

26. Another dead T-54 in the city. This photo, inscribed by General Hollingsworth, courtesy of Pham, vnafmamn.

27. A Soviet-supplied 57 mm twin-barreled antiaircraft weapon killed in the city. This ZSU-57-2 was one of the many threats faced by aircrews. Photo by Colonel Walter Ulmer, courtesy of Carruthers, *The Battle of An Loc: A Massive Convergence of Forces.*

Loc part of the Easter Offensive, another that 118 armor vehicles of all types littered the landscape.[3]

From 2 April when the enemy crossed the Cambodian border until An Loc was declared secure, South Vietnamese units on that portion of the battlefield suffered some 5,400 casualties that included 2,300 killed or missing. South Vietnamese units tasked with opening Highway 13 suffered an additional 4,000 men killed or wounded.[4] There are no good numbers for civilian casualties during the battle.

29

Off with the Old and on with the New

On the first morning I woke up in Colonel Taylor's bunker, which turned out to be 20 May, a soldier told me an American helicopter was en route and intended to slip into the city. I needed to get ready to go and it didn't take long. I was happy to find that Major Jack Todd, who had first welcomed me to Team 162, and Lieutenant Pep McPhillips, the shot-down FAC, were also planning to leave. Lieutenant Colonel Ed Benedit, an advisor with the 5th ARVN Division, succeeded in joining us. I sought out Colonel Taylor and gave him a .38 snub-nose I'd carried in my pants pocket for several years. While my back-up gun might not be anything he'd need, giving it to him made me feel a little bit better.

The four who were leaving met at the foot of the stairs before climbing out of the bunker. Once in the open we took turns jogging past the burned-out T-54 to the helicopter pad, about a hundred yards through clutter and junk. It was blistering hot and the sweat immediately began to run. Four seriously wounded Vietnamese soldiers had already been carried to the pad by the time we arrived. They were strapped onto stretchers and looked tiny and sick. Artillery rounds were whistling into the city, and the explosions caused me to flinch and duck. Several rounds came screaming into our immediate neighborhood, and my American buddies and I crawled into an empty concrete drain pipe lying discarded at the edge of the pad. Getting wounded or killed was still a very real possibility. There weren't any options for the Vietnamese who remained strapped to their stretchers. As I lay in the drain pipe it crossed my mind that I'd probably never be in that kind of situation again, provided we were able to get out of town. I began to count the incoming rounds.

For the next ten or fifteen minutes I stretched out in the dirt with a pair of worn and scuffed jungle boots in my face. I counted to fifty, and then I gave up as shells continued to impact around the city. I decided to restart my count and limit it to just those rounds close enough to be dangerous. The time dragged in a haze of sweat and anxiety as we continued to wait for the helicopter. The only solace I could take from the situation was that the soldiers on the stretchers were even more exposed than we were in our drain pipe. Then suddenly and without any warning an American Huey helicopter came roaring across the treetops from the south and twisted around to land hard on the pad in a swirl of dirt and rubbish. I forgot my count as I scrambled onto the steel mesh of the pad.

Within a few seconds the wounded soldiers were moved from their stretchers to the floor of the aircraft. My three American comrades and I climbed in and got seat belts cinched up in less time than it takes to tell. The rotors had not slowed and the helicopter immediately lifted off in a small cyclone of flying dirt. As we cleared the neighborhood I leaned out the open door for one last look at An Loc. Staring back at the sweltering town I saw five or six dirty puffs of smoke blossom on the pad we'd just left. The enemy had evidently used that location to register several mortars and once they woke to the fact that a helicopter had flown in they started firing. They missed us by about ten seconds.

As a footnote to our departure experience, North Vietnamese shelling was never completely turned off in the An Loc area. Some five weeks later, on 9 July, Brigadier General Richard Tallman, who had only recently replaced Brigadier General John McGiffert as General Hollingsworth's deputy, was mortally wounded and four members of his party were killed on that same pad. They had flown in to inspect the town and were shelled before they could get under cover. General Tallman and two other Americans who were wounded in the incident were immediately evacuated to the 3rd Field Hospital in Saigon. The two wounded soldiers, Major Joe Hallum and Captain James Willbanks, survived; General Tallman died on the operating table. That event was a grim reminder of the enemy's continuing dangerous reach. In fact one more American life was forfeited before the book was finally closed on the battle of An Loc. Lieutenant Colonel William Nolde was killed near the city by enemy shell fire on 27 January 1973, while serving as the province senior advisor. Colonel Nolde was officially recognized as the last American soldier killed in action in South Vietnam before the Paris-brokered ceasefire went into effect.

I didn't see any tracers fired in our direction as we barreled across the southeastern outskirts of the city, and I don't think we took any fire during the twenty-minute flight to the brigade's logistics base at Lai Khe. The flight was at treetop level and full throttle, which gave the enemy very little time to react as we tore past. It lasted just long enough for me to begin to believe I might yet survive the whole bloody experience.

Our courageous helicopter crew deposited us at the airbase on the outskirts of Lai Khe. A Vietnamese ambulance was waiting for the wounded, and Colonel Benedit was met by his contact. An American airborne advisor was sitting in a jeep at the edge of the pad to greet the rest of us. Before I jumped out of the helicopter I thanked the door gunners and both pilots for putting their lives on the line to pick us up. They responded with a grin and a big thumbs-up. The advisor's tent was close by and within five minutes Jack, Pep, and I had a cold sodas in our hands as we marveled at how normal life was on the base. Everyone was walking around in the open, seemingly unconcerned about being suddenly struck dead. It was novel to see people going about their business without scurrying like fugitives. It seemed like a very long time since I'd enjoyed a sense of normality and it took some getting used to. Until recently the home of numerous U.S. Army and Air Force units, there were now very few Americans in evidence on the Lai Khe airbase.

We borrowed the advisor's jeep and hit the road south to Saigon. The drive was uneventful and we were waved through Tan Son Nhut's main gate by midafternoon. Again, I was deeply impressed by the routine pace of life everyone outside our jeep took for granted. Our first stop was to deliver Pep to his FAC squadron where a welcome-home celebration was already underway. Champagne corks were popping and air force party hats were available to one and all. Jack and I stood out like embarrassing eccentrics in our grimy tiger-stripes, battered steel helmets, and weapons hanging on straps. Before taking our leave we did accept a flute of bubbly from a well-manicured air force colonel sporting a tailored flight suit that matched his sparkling blue eyes. He was polite and vaguely solicitous although careful to stay at arms-length. I'd noticed Pep was still limping but his injury was quickly forgotten when the happiness began to flow. Pep recently told me he discovered the ankle was fractured when it was x-rayed at 3rd Field in Saigon. If the airborne advisors had known of the fracture we would have given him positive points for being a stoic, but I fear he would have lost those points for making a sloppy parachute landing to begin with.

Once our FAC had been delivered Jack and I drove to the Vietnamese Airborne Division's compound to check in. Several Americans welcomed us back with handshakes and an update on the status of other units and advisors. I got a stack of mail and then I was ready for a shower, a decent meal, and some sleep.

The drive downtown was a reintroduction to Saigon's frantic traffic and swarming streets, and suddenly I was back in my dingy but reassuringly quiet refuge at the Missouri BOQ. It was so quiet and peaceful, and I was alone for the first time in months. I hadn't really anticipated being there so soon and I felt disconnected from the reality of actually being back in that room. I sat on the edge of the bed for a few minutes to think it over as I pulled off my tiger stripes and worn-out jungle boots. The fatigues were beyond salvaging and joined the boots in the garbage. I got into the shower and stayed there, soaping and rinsing, soaping and rinsing, for the next hour. The realities of my deliverance finally began to really sink in as the red dirt went down the drain. I had won the lottery.

Four days after flying out of An Loc I walked off an airliner in San Francisco and caught a connecting flight for South Dakota. Those rapid-fire changes in my life, from living with the 5th Airborne Battalion's command group and the devastation of the battle to the peace and quiet of small-town America in less than a week, were beyond comprehension. My parents were shocked at my physical condition and my mother immediately set to work making me healthy. My folks must have been equally nonplussed by my mental and emotional state, but they were very considerate and let me find my own way back into the rhythm of daily life at home. It was just as well we didn't try to discuss the specifics of what I'd recently left. Beyond the obvious and the superficial I wouldn't have been able to explain or begin to describe what I'd been involved in.

I moved into the basement rather than the empty second-floor bedroom my brothers and I occupied when we were growing up. My parents slept in an adjoining bedroom upstairs and I knew my restlessness would bother my mother. Besides, the basement was cool and solid and safe and I could slip out the back door to walk the streets when sleep wasn't possible. During the pre-dawn hours of a summer morning my little prairie hometown was blessedly peaceful and quiet. The night air was wonderfully cool, beautifully clean, and indescribably sweet. I found the dangerous past and the serene present equally difficult to get my arms around. I certainly didn't recognize those unsettled nocturnal moments as a harbinger of a lifelong nagging disquiet, but I've gotten very few unassisted night's sleep since then.

Something else I didn't fully appreciate that summer was how the peoples of Indochina were going to suffer once America's retreat from the region began to really take hold. My frustration and anger concerning how the war ended didn't come into a better focus until later in the 1970s when some of the results of America's abandonment started washing up in refugee camps throughout the region. While an untold number of boat people died at sea trying to escape their communist conquerors, more than three million Vietnamese eventually found refuge in foreign lands. Roughly half were resettled in the United States, the very country that had sold them down the river. The irony was not lost on those who were forced to make a new life in a totally foreign and largely indifferent society. At about the same time Americans began to learn something about the horrific Reeducation Camps established by the Vietnamese communists once they took control. Pol Pot, locally known as Brother Number One, and his comrades were also hard at work in the Cambodian killing fields. The results of their appalling program also started making the news.

It has taken many years for me to better understand some of the personal ramifications of my combat experience. I was resilient enough to make the transition from war to peace, at least to the extent I probably appeared normal to most people most of the time. But I remained stuck in a lonely kind of place I could not share. As an example, for years I stayed on sidewalks or the street as much as possible, cringing at the thought of walking in the grass and stepping on a mine. When faced with the choice of strolling across a lawn, to include university campuses and city parks, or taking the longer way around on a hard surface, I took the less direct route. I fully appreciated how irrational that prickly sensation was and never mentioned it to anyone. Who could possibly understand? But no matter, I was more comfortable with the safer path. Over time I started to walk around a bit more like a normal person although I'll admit, particularly when I'm out alone, the longer route can still be the preferred choice.

Electronic entertainment was never big on my list of things to do, and I soon found that even the most highly touted and popular movies and television programs left me feeling agitated and impatient. I was bored by the inconsequential story lines and canned emotions that others seemed to take seriously. So much of popular culture struck me as pathetically shallow, shrill, without substance or value. I spent hours exploring the frustrations of reentry into American society with friends I trusted. Some seemed to agree while others thought I was overly critical.

It wasn't easy to fit back in. I felt unsure of myself and couldn't seem to trust the tone, to relax and join the fun. I'd forgotten how to participate as a light-hearted member of the group. Invited and welcomed by others whose company I enjoyed, people who found humor in innocent things, I felt left on the edge of the circle, withdrawn, too serious. I'd become an observer, didn't seem to mesh, couldn't find the easy rhythm of belonging like before. With time I've learned that I'm not my best as a loner and work at finding a place, but I'm sensitive to what's been lost.

On a more somber note, for many years I would occasionally feel myself slipping away from the reality of the moment and into another kind of ill-defined space where my dead buddies were waiting. They were all there, standing together as I had last seen them, looking at me, silent and just beyond my reach. Those visits never happened as a dream when I was asleep, only when I was awake, and we didn't speak. I was not surprised or upset to see them—they were all my friends. At those moments I felt desperately sad and guilty beyond telling. I had let them go on ahead and I had stayed behind. They had not sought to leave me, but they were on the other side and now I could only join them by my own hand. Over time those moments began to occur less often and my thoughts of catching up became less compelling—the urgency somehow not as necessary to consider or act on.

In a more positive vein I've begun to make a conscious effort to learn and remember people's names. The reason for not previously fixing names in my mind was not mental laziness. I've known for a long time it was an outgrowth of my combat experience starting with the first tour in the 101st Airborne Division. Young platoon leaders are expected to know their men, their histories, their needs, and certainly their names. When I arrived in Vietnam I worked hard to meet that standard, at least until the volume of casualties began to teach me the limits of my ability to protect those in my care. It didn't take long to learn I could not satisfy the most basic responsibility of a small unit leader. Despite my best efforts I could not keep my soldiers safe, uninjured, alive.

During that first tour I don't recall many soldiers completing a year in the field unwounded, to include myself. I don't have any idea how many men cycled through my platoon or through the company during the first twelve months I served in Vietnam. I did keep track of the officers; as a group they represented a more manageable number to record and I have their names in a rain-stained notebook I carried at the time. An airborne rifle company was authorized six officers (company commander, executive officer, and four platoon leaders) although as I recall the company was seldom at full strength. Nineteen officers were assigned to C Company, 2nd Battalion, 327th Airborne Infantry, between June 1967 and June 1968. All but three were wounded or killed. As time went on I simply stopped learning names and for years called people by their rank or Sir, or fell back on Buddy or Partner, or if they wore a skirt, Honey. More recently, however, I've begun to believe that folks who have become an important part of my life might not leave unexpectedly, and I've started acting on that encouraging notion.

With the passing years I've also tried to become a more patient person, allowing myself to live the time I've been given, embracing those who love

me here, flawed person that I am. But I do know the day will arrive when
my buddies and I will stand together again. For my part I will try to explain
how my life has been incomplete since they left and not going with them was
my fate. I will not, however, be able to explain why America's leaders chose
to make their deaths pointless, a futility, while breaking the hearts of those
who survived.

30
In Retrospect

I returned to America angry and discouraged, suspecting the South Vietnamese had entered a downward spiral that would eventually end in their destruction. I was also becoming painfully aware that I'd been led down the garden path and left hanging as this country's leaders did their deal with the enemy. It was time for me to reevaluate those treasured principles I'd learned at home, those fundamental reasons underlying my commitment to serve as an officer of the United States.

First of all I decided if I was going to be a professional soldier I had to get the basics right. While I might not always agree with national policy I had taken an oath to support and defend the Constitution, pledging true faith and allegiance to my military chain-of-command and the nation's commander-in-chief. I reserved the option of resigning my commission if I was ever required to support a morally repugnant order, but in fact that kind of situation never occurred. All that aside, I had finally come to realize my vision of America as a shining city on a hill demanded a serious reality check. While my sense of patriotism hadn't shifted I had learned this nation's political leadership was sometimes less than what I'd been taught to expect.

The final day of reckoning for the South Vietnamese arrived on 30 April 1975, when the communists drove their tanks into Saigon. A modest flotilla of U.S. Navy ships was off shore to accept the Vietnamese who could flee right then, but the thing was over. As I watched gassy television personalities blathering on about those last frantic Americans scrambling off the Saigon rooftops, my thoughts turned to the paratroopers of the Vietnamese Airborne Division. There were certainly no imbedded news personalities available to trivialize their final agonies. My heart was with those tough, dedicated, and uncomplaining soldiers. I was absolutely sure they would battle their enemies to the very last, which is exactly what they did.

In my mind's eye I could see them on unknown and uncelebrated battle-fields, fighting on without any hope of victory or reprieve. Those men would be true to themselves as they embraced their final mission. In 1972 I had seen them throw off their steel helmets as their positions were being over-whelmed; I was sure they would be wearing their maroon paratrooper berets when the axe fell this time, too.

In fact, several of the airborne battalions refused to surrender with the rest of the South Vietnamese army and moved into the countryside to con-tinue the fight until they were eventually cornered and destroyed. A number of airborne officers committed suicide rather than be taken by their com-munist enemies.[1]

I know as well as any man and better than most how combat soldiers are willing to serve their nation and sacrifice for their buddies. I also know how meaningful their struggles and their deaths are for all who have earned true membership in that demanding brotherhood. While those of us who re-sponded to the call were prepared to bear any burden and meet any hardship, America's policy makers referenced a different dynamic, less predictable and less accountable. After initially providing near-unanimous support backed by massive funding to fuel the energetic enthusiasms and profligate excesses this country visited on Indochina, our leaders eventually turned their backs and simply abandoned the whole enormous effort. So the fight that America pursued for years, that cost a mountain of treasure and a legion of lives, simply became null. Null and void, at least to our leaders.

Slowly and painfully I've come to accept that America's war in Vietnam, that great crusade I and tens of thousands of others embraced with dedi-cation, turned out to have foundations built on shifting sands. The clarion call to action proved to be a siren's false promise, and it has been very hard for me to accept that I misplaced my trust, that I was so naïve for so long. While coming to terms with that sad realization I have also had to accept another painful truth—every one of those 58,260 names inscribed on The Vietnam Veterans Memorial represents a soldier whose death, in the final analysis, served no real purpose. They died following their orders and do-ing their duty, but their sacrifice lost any larger purpose or more significant value when America's leaders reversed their promises and abandoned the field to the enemy. In that sense each and every one of those faithful soldiers, my comrades in a specious war, died in vain.

I've visited that Wall several times, during the day when people are search-ing for names and leaving memorabilia and late at night when all is silent. My visits have been a wrenching reminder of what was lost, and it devas-tates me. The tears run and I can't stop weeping until I've gotten away from the place. That's why those shiny black slabs with their relentless rows of memory evoke such wrenching anguish for veterans as well as all the others who loved those lost soldiers. Despite all the political rhetoric, the commitment and suffering of those abandoned soldiers, recorded for all to ponder on that somber monument to failure, had no more value to this nation's leaders than did the other long-held promises that were so recklessly broken.

And that brings me back to my restless nights. It's almost 4:00 in the morning and while no danger seems to lurk in the backyard a residual sense of grief, a nagging feeling of irretrievable loss, troubles my mind. For most Americans the realities of the Vietnam War, the terrible sacrifices and the final betrayal of trust, have faded into obscurity.

That whole episode has become a paragraph in a history book, ancient history as little understood or appreciated as the Peloponnesian Wars. But even while I relock the bedroom door and seek out my loving Chulan I know that for some of us the pain of that great sacrifice, that great multilayered double-cross, will continue to fall drop by drop upon our hearts. As I sink back into the comfort of our bed I pray that perhaps, with a generous gift of God's healing grace, the despair for all we lost might eventually be transformed into something more like wisdom. Perhaps.

Epilogue

North Vietnam's 1972 Easter Offensive presented an immediate and extremely serious threat to South Vietnam; it was also a harbinger of things to come. While the North Vietnamese enemy did not accomplish their primary objectives in the spring of 1972, they did go to school on a number of lessons that became operative three years later when they kicked off their next offensive and succeeded in overrunning the country. Perhaps the most important lesson they learned during the Easter Offensive was to wait until the Americans were well and truly out of the way. The brutally effective advisor/airpower team the North Vietnamese encountered in 1972 was a major factor in frustrating their Easter Offensive objectives, and without that American presence on the battlefield they were able to successfully steamroller the South Vietnamese in the spring of 1975.

More germane to this story, the North Vietnamese attack to capture the provincial capital of An Loc arrived as a massive and shocking surprise. The scope and lethality of the battle presented a major test for both the South Vietnamese and the Americans engaged in the battle. The defenders of An Loc took on the enemy with magnificent courage and gritty perseverance, and I would like to provide a brief update concerning how life unfolded for a few of them following the battle.

Major General James Hollingsworth continued to serve as the commanding general of the Third Regional Assistance Command throughout the course of the Easter Offensive and was subsequently promoted to the rank of lieutenant general. General Hollingsworth entered service during World War II, was retired in 1976, and passed away on 2 March 2010. He was one of the most highly decorated soldiers in the history of the United States Army. Awarded the Distinguished Service Cross three times during the course of his career,

General Hollingsworth also earned four Silver Stars and six Purple Hearts as well as numerous other awards and decorations.

Brigadier General Le Van Hung, who commanded the 5th ARVN Division during the battle, was promoted to major general and was the deputy commander of IV Corps in April 1975 when he was notified the South Vietnamese military had been ordered to capitulate. After saying farewell to his wife, General Hung shot himself rather than surrender. His commander, Major General Nguyen Khoa Nam, also refused to put himself in the hands of his enemies and committed suicide in his office.

Colonel Le Nguyen Vy, the 5th ARVN Division deputy commander during the battle, was promoted to brigadier general and assumed command of the division when General Hung was reassigned. General Vy was still in command of the division when Saigon fell. He committed suicide rather than surrender.

Colonel Le Quang Luong, the 1st Airborne brigade commander throughout the Easter Offensive, was promoted to brigadier general and took command of the Airborne Division. He remained the division commander until Saigon fell and then immigrated to the United States, passing away in 2007.

Colonel Ho Ngoc Can commanded the task force that, supported by the 6th Airborne Battalion, pushed up Highway 13 and made the first link-up with the An Loc garrison. In 1975 he was serving as a province chief in IV Corps. When Saigon fell he refused to surrender and continued to conduct combat operations until his units ran out of ammunition. When eventually captured, Colonel Can was taken to Can Tho, the province capital, where he was executed on the city's soccer field.

Colonel Walter Ulmer, senior advisor to the 5th ARVN Division, completed his tour in Vietnam and was subsequently assigned to West Point as the commandant of cadets. He later commanded the 3rd Armored Division and retired in 1985 as a lieutenant general. General Ulmer remains actively involved in a range of leadership projects as well as the West Point Association of Graduates.

Lieutenant Colonel Art Taylor, senior advisor to the 1st Airborne Brigade, completed his tour in Vietnam and was promoted to the rank of colonel soon after returning to the United States. He retired several years later and has subsequently passed away.

Lieutenant Colonel Nguyen Chi Hieu, the 5th Airborne Battalion commander, was promoted to colonel after the battle and resettled in the United States following the surrender of South Vietnam.

Major Pham Van Huan, the commander of the 81st Airborne Ranger Group during the battle, was a colonel in 1975. Following the surrender of the South Vietnamese army he was incarcerated in a series of North Vietnamese Re-education Camps for years before being released. Colonel Huan now lives in the United States.

Major Jack Todd completed his tour with Team 162 and was promoted to lieutenant colonel after returning to the United States. He retired to his home state of Georgia in 1980 where he and his family continue to make their home. Jack taught science and math programs at the secondary level for years before retiring a second time.

Lieutenant Ross Kelly was awarded the Distinguished Service Cross for his actions while serving with the 6th Airborne Battalion during the defense and evacuation of the hilltop firebase southeast of An Loc. Visit the Legion of Valor Web site to read his award citation. Ross stayed in the army and re-tired as a colonel before settling in northern Virginia, where he established and operated a security company. He passed away on 25 August, 2011.

Lieutenant Winston Cover was also awarded the Distinguished Service Cross for his actions while serving as the senior advisor with the 8th Air-borne Battalion during the defense of the southern approaches to An Loc. Visit the Legion of Valor Web site to read his award citation. Winston con-tinued to serve following the Vietnam War and retired as a lieutenant colonel.

Lieutenant Pep McPhillips returned to the United States and continued his aviation career that included transitioning into A-10 Warthogs before re-tiring as a lieutenant colonel in 1990. He played pro golf for several years and became a rules official for both the United States Golf Association and the National Collegiate Athletic Association. Pep remains active with both or-ganizations; he and his family make their home in South Carolina.

Lieutenant Bill Carruthers transitioned into B-52s after leaving Vietnam and then was a pilot for U.S. Airways before retiring in 2002. Bill and his family live in North Carolina where he has established an extraordinary col-lection of materials related to the An Loc battle. Bill's Web site, http://www .anloc.org/, showcases the depth of his archives as well as the breadth of his devoted community of admirers.

Platoon Sergeant Ronald McCauley was one of the most capable and pro-fessional noncommissioned officers I ever worked with. He began his long and distinguished service as a soldier in the British Parachute Regiment and after immigrating to the United States became an American paratrooper. Ron always knew what was required and then did it thoroughly and com-pletely. He continued his service after leaving Vietnam and eventually retired with the rank of sergeant major.

28. A highly decorated Vietnamese paratrooper, photo courtesy of Pham, vnafmamn.

Appendix I

During the course of the battle for An Loc both sides fed units into the fight. The enemy initially attempted to overrun the city with the following formations:

9th Viet Cong Division
    271st Regiment
    272nd Regiment
    95C Regiment
69th Artillery Division
    42nd Artillery Regiment
    208th Rocket Regiment
    271st Anti-Aircraft Regiment
203rd Tank Regiment of two battalions plus elements of the 202nd Tank
    Regiment
429th Sapper Group

At the same time additional North Vietnamese units cut Highway 13 south of An Loc. They included the following:

7th North Vietnamese Division
    141st Regiment
    165th Regiment
    209th Regiment
    101st Independent Regiment
Elements of the 69th Artillery Division

As the battle progressed and the North Vietnamese became desperate to overrun the city they reinforced with the following units. Their troop strength in the immediate vicinity of An Loc then totaled approximately 36,000 soldiers.

9th Viet Cong Division
   271st Regiment
   272nd Regiment
   95C Regiment
5th Viet Cong Division (moved down from the earlier Loc Ninh battle)
   174th Regiment
   275th Regiment
   E6 Regiment
   141st Regiment (moved up from Highway 13)
   165th Regiment (moved up from Highway 13)
69th Artillery Division
   42nd Artillery Regiment
   208th Rocket Regiment
   271st Anti-Aircraft Regiment
203rd Tank Regiment of two battalions plus elements of the 202nd Tank
   Regiment
429th Sapper Group

Capturing the border town of Loc Ninh was the first mission for those North Vietnamese units invading from Cambodia. That battle occurred from 4–8 April, and the following South Vietnamese units were destroyed before the battle moved on to An Loc.

Two infantry battalions of the 5th Division's 9th Regiment
   1st Armored Cavalry Squadron
   74th Border Ranger Battalion
   Task Force 52, comprised of two infantry battalions, lost their vehicles and heavy weapons but approximately half the soldiers assigned moved across country and joined the An Loc defenses.

At the height of the battle for An Loc the South Vietnamese defenders totaled approximately 5,800 soldiers and included the following organizations:

5th Infantry Division
   7th Regiment minus one battalion
   8th Regiment
   Task Force 52 consisting of two infantry battalions

3rd Ranger Group

1st Airborne Brigade

    5th Airborne Battalion

    6th Airborne Battalion (Destroyed on the firebase southeast of An Loc but rebuilt around the survivors of that fight. The battalion then rejoined the battle, fighting as part of the force that was reopening Highway 13. Soldiers of the 6th Airborne Battalion were the first to eventually reach An Loc as part of the task force coming from the south.)

    8th Airborne Battalion

81st Airborne Ranger Group (battalion size unit)

Two Regional Force/Popular Force infantry battalions

Although the South Vietnamese were unable to add to their troop strength in An Loc after the 1st Airborne Brigade and the 81st Airborne Ranger Group were inserted, they did increase the size of the force that was fighting to re-open Highway 13. The following units were engaged when the city was eventually relieved:

21st Infantry Division

    31st Regiment

    32nd Regiment

    33rd Regiment

    15th Regiment

    46th Regiment

    9th Armored Cavalry Regiment

    The reconstituted 8th Airborne Battalion

Appendix 2

'Thunder Road' Paved With Blood

By HUGH A. MULLIGAN

CHON THANH, Vietnam (AP)—"What's wrong with this girl?" asked Capt. Mike McDermott, holding up a *Pacific Stars & Stripes* that showed Raquel Welch in fulsome cleavage at the Academy Awards ceremony.

He was hard to hear over the blam-blam of howitzers firing at an enemy machine gun somewhere nearby in the jungle scrubs.

"Ain't nothing wrong with that girl," answered the major advising the ARVN—Army of the Republic of Vietnam—artillery. "Nothing at all."

"Good," said the captain, raising his voice to contend with a helicopter whirling down to take out some wounded. "Then there's nothing wrong with me. So far."

McDermott, from Highmore, S.D., squatted at a field telephone in the corrugated sewer pipe serving as the front line command post on Highway 13, Vietnam's Thunder Road.

A four-year man in the Nam, having extended twice on previous tours with the 101st Airborne, the captain took issue with a visitor who called Highway 13 "interesting."

"That's rear echelon talk," he corrected between telephone squawks telling why he couldn't get more air strikes and what had become of the water he ordered yesterday for his men. "It's not interesting. It's dangerous. Goddam dangerous."

He found no argument in this quarter. On the drive up from Saigon this reporter and two other AP men hit the floorboards when a B40 rocket tried to zero in on our hired car and an AK47 rifle pop-popped from only a few hundred yards away. The driver jammed the accelerator down and careened up the road with only his eyeballs showing above the dashboard.

Only a few miles back, Route 13 had been a happy chaos of three-wheel taxicabs, oxcarts, droning motor bikes, overcrowded provincial buses, mobile noodle restaurants, and women in conical hats hunkered down before brimming baskets of fruits and vegetables at roadside markets.

Now the wide road through the rubber plantations and stretches of scrub jungle was empty and menacing except for an occasional lumbering armored column. Asia's teeming tide of life recedes and vanishes in the path of advancing armies.

Just around the bend from where the rocketeer took aim at our blue Buick, the 21st ARVN Division from the Mekong Delta was strung out in a long line. Moving up to relieve An Loc, 60 miles from Saigon, the column was held up by the fighting at Fire Base No Name, where McDermott begged for water and air strikes. Under a blazing noon sun, the troops squatted in the shade of their armored vehicles, longing for a nice cool rice paddie to wade in.

A derrick truck came down the road dragging another shell-blasted Russian tank.

"Soon every village in Vietnam will have a Russian tank to display, like Civil War cannons on the courthouse lawns back home," said an American sergeant.

Highway 13, Indochina's rubber road, runs from the outskirts of Saigon deep into Cambodia and is a living road map—or perhaps a death map—of the war that won't go away.

Here is grown the finest rubber in the world, with whole stands set aside for racing car tires. Beginning at Lai Khe, halfway to the Cambodian border, the plantations are immense, some of them 75 miles square and employing 20,000 men.

For a reporter coming back to Vietnam almost every year since 1965, it's Deja Vu Valley. You've seen it all before. The tall orderly stands of rubber trees look shady and cool and peaceful. They're not.

They meet war's specifications for slaughter.

Splendid cover against planes, perfect protection for ambushers crouched behind the trees to fire down the long straight rows at the exposed highway.

Here in 1964 and '65, ARVN regiments were massacred in slaughterhouse scenes of running blood and dripping latex. Then the U.S. 1st Div., the Big Red One, arrived in July 1965, and staked out the rubber plantation country and the surrounding scrubby jungles of War Zones C and D as its own Charlie-hunting preserve.

One morning in summer at a place called Bau Bang, the Big Red One left 138 Viet Cong bodies to simmer in a row along Route 13 as a warning of things to come. The warning didn't take. A week later the 3rd Brigade Hq. in the Lai Khe Plantation was furiously attacked with heavy losses on both sides.

A year later the Big Red One had a howitzer named Bau Bang and another named Ben Cat, both firing into the jungles in those directions. Pacification in these parts came out of the barrel of a gun.

The 1st Div. built an orphanage at Ben Cat in honor of Sgt. Arthur McMellon, a mess cook who was kind to kids and bought the farm one day in a mine blast under his jeep on Thunder Road.

The division went home two years ago and the orphanage, like its base camps, was Vietnamized. The sergeant's name was obliterated. Now, in the renewed fighting, it's been abandoned. Except for an occasional helmet out in the bush or rusting tins of C-rations, time and the jungles have all but wiped out the American presence.

There were days of hope and high promise on Route 13 over the years. In the Spring of 1967 the Big Red One cleared the road all the way to the border, and the first big convoy of rubber moved down to the Saigon docks from the Terre Rouge plantation. RMK, the big construction firm, widened and improved the road, and last fall for the first time in seven years Vietnam began exporting rubber.

Now no one knows what will happen along Thunder Road, least of all the men fighting there.

"All I know is what's happening 100 yards in front of me, and that ain't good," said McDermott. "I'd give anything

Capt. Mike McDermott is an adviser with a South Vietnamese Airborne column moving up "dangerous" Route 13.   (AP)

for a look at the 8th Division war map . . . anything except that leave coming up in Honolulu next month."

The day before, a shower of rockets killed four men and injured a dozen at Fire Base No Name. Another burst came in today, but the camp's busy bulldozer had built the bunkers up higher.

"That's our most valuable fighting weapon," the captain said, watching the blade push up another defense barrier of mud and sand.

After the rocket barrage, a helicopter came in to take out a North Vietnamese captured two days before. His head and arms were swathed in bandages, and his ankles were in handcuffs. With him went an ARVN soldier, crying softly under a hood of bloodied bandages.

At the cross roads in Ben Cat, a war veteran came crawling across the macadam on stumps of knees and knobs of elbows, his beggar's bowl pinned to the shirt of his faded ARVN fatigues.

29. Reprinted courtesy of *Pacific Stars & Stripes*/Heritage Microfilm.

Appendix 3

Date of Shoot Down	Aircraft Type
5 April	USA AH-1G Cobra Helicopter
9 April	VNAF UH-1H Huey Helicopter
11 April	USA AH-1G Cobra Helicopter
12 April	VNAF CH-47 Chinook Helicopter
15 April	VNAF C-123 Provider
18 April	USAF C-130 Hercules
19 April	VNAF C-123 Provider
25 April	USAF C-130 Hercules
1 May	USA AH-1G Cobra Helicopter
2 May	USAF AC-119K Stinger Gunship
3 May	USAF C-130 Hercules
9 May	VNAF CH-47 Chinook Helicopter
11 May	VNAF A1-E Skyraider
	VNAF UH-1H Huey Helicopter
	Two USAF O-2 Skymaster FACs
	USA AH-1G Cobra Helicopter

This was the aircraft crewed by Captain Rodney Strobridge and Captain Robert Williams, shot down by a SA-7 missile while providing support to the 5th Airborne Battalion on the south side of An Loc.

USAF A-37 Dragonfly

This aircraft was piloted by 1st Lieutenant Michael Blassie, whose remains were initially interred at the Tomb of the Unknowns in Arlington National Cemetery before being returned to his family.

13 May	VNAF A1-E Skyraider
	VNAF UH-1H Huey Helicopter
14 May	USAF A1-E Skyraider

USAF O-2 Skymaster

This was the aircraft piloted by Lieutenant Pep McPhillips, whose drop-in was a surprise to both him and the soldiers of the 5th Airborne Battalion.

24 May	USA AH-1G Cobra Helicopter
8 June	USA UH-1H Huey Medivac Helicopter
13 June	USA UH-1H Huey Helicopter
17 June	USA AH-1G Cobra Helicopter
20 June	USA AH-1G Cobra Helicopter
24 June	USA AH-1G Cobra Helicopter

Appendix 4

THE UNITED STATES OF AMERICA

TO ALL WHO SHALL SEE THESE PRESENTS, GREETING:

THIS IS TO CERTIFY THAT
THE PRESIDENT OF THE UNITED STATES OF AMERICA
AUTHORIZED BY CONGRESS
HAS AWARDED

THE DISTINGUISHED SERVICE CROSS

(FIRST OAK LEAF CLUSTER)

TO

CAPTAIN MICHAEL A. MC DERMOTT, INFANTRY
UNITED STATES ARMY

FOR

EXTRAORDINARY HEROISM IN ACTION

IN THE REPUBLIC OF VIETNAM DURING THE PERIOD 16 APRIL 1972 TO 20 MAY 1972

GIVEN UNDER MY HAND IN THE CITY OF WASHINGTON
THIS   17TH   DAY OF   OCTOBER   1972

FRED C. WEYAND
General, United States Army

SECRETARY OF THE ARMY

30. Citation for the Distinguished Service Cross (First Oak Leaf Cluster) awarded to Captain Mike McDermott for actions during the battle for An Loc.

GENERAL ORDERS   17 October 1972
NUMBER   2442

AWARD OF THE DISTINGUISHED SERVICE CROSS

TC 439. The following AWARD is announced.

MCDERMOTT, MICHAEL A.   CAPTAIN INFANTRY United States Army,
Airborne Division Assistance Team, Army Advisory Group, APO 96307
Awarded: Distinguished Service Cross (First Oak Leaf Cluster).
Date of action: 16 April 1972 to 20 May 1972
Theater: Republic of Vietnam
Authority: By direction of the President, under the provisions of the Act
     of Congress, approved 25 July 1963
Reason: For extraordinary heroism in connection with military operations
     involving conflict with an armed hostile force in the Republic of
     Vietnam: Captain Michael A. McDermott distinguished himself while
     serving as Senior Advisor to the 5th Airborne Battalion, Airborne
     Division, Army of the Republic of Vietnam, during the period 16
     April 1972 to 20 May 1972 in the besieged provincial capital of
     An Loc. During this period, the 5th Airborne Battalion received
     daily attacks by numerically superior enemy forces during which
     Captain McDermott continuously exposed himself to the enemy fire
     and directed devastating airstrikes to turn back their assaults.
     When the embattled 5th Airborne Battalion was ordered to disengage
     from the enemy, he remained with rear elements of the unit and pro-
     tected the movement to a more advantageous position by again direct-
     ing numerous airstrikes. The enemy then launched a massive mortar
     and ground assault supported by tanks. During this attack, Captain
     McDermott disregarded his personal safety by moving from one posi-
     tion to another under a fusillade of enemy fire and adjusted air-
     strikes to eventually ward off the assault after eight hours of
     continuous fighting. His determination and heroism in the face
     of overwhelming odds served as inspiration to the weary para-
     troopers and rallied them to hold their positions. Captain
     McDermott's personal bravery and devotion to duty were in keeping
     with the highest traditions of the military service and reflect
     great credit upon himself and the United States Army.

GENERAL ORDERS NUMBER   2442   dated 17 Oct 72   , DEPARTMENT OF THE
ARMY, Headquarters, United States Army Vietnam/MACV Support Command, APO San
Francisco 96375 (Cont)

FOR THE COMMANDER:

HAROLD H. DUNWOODY
Brigadier General, US Army
Chief of Staff

R. W. HORNBUCKLE
Colonel, AGC
Adjutant General

31. Official orders for the Distinguished Service Cross (First Oak Leaf Cluster).

THE UNITED STATES OF AMERICA

TO ALL WHO SHALL SEE THESE PRESENTS, GREETING:

THIS IS TO CERTIFY THAT

THE PRESIDENT OF THE UNITED STATES OF AMERICA
AUTHORIZED BY ACT OF CONGRESS JULY 9, 1918
HAS AWARDED

THE SILVER STAR

TO

CAPTAIN MICHAEL A. McDERMOTT,   INFANTRY, UNITED STATES ARMY

FOR

GALLANTRY IN ACTION

IN THE REPUBLIC OF VIETNAM ON 20 APRIL 1972

GIVEN UNDER MY HAND IN THE CITY OF WASHINGTON

THIS   19th   DAY OF   JULY   1972

FRED C. WEYAND
General, United States Army

Robert J. Froehlke
SECRETARY OF THE ARMY

32. Citation for the Silver Star awarded to Captain Mike McDermott for actions during the battle for An Loc.

HEADQUARTERS
UNITED STATES MILITARY ASSISTANCE COMMAND, VIETNAM
APO San Francisco 96222

GENERAL ORDERS   19 July 1972
NUMBER   1967

AWARD OF THE SILVER STAR

1. TC 439. The following AWARD is announced.

McDERMOTT, MICHAEL A.   CPT INF USA ABN Div adv det, Adv
Tm 162, HQ MACV, APO 96307
  Awarded: Silver Star
  Dates of service: 20 April 1972
  Theater: Republic of Vietnam
  Authority: By direction of the President under the provisions of
         the Act of Congress, approved 9 July 1918
  Reason: For gallantry in action: Captain McDermott distinguished
         himself by gallantry in action on 20 April 1972 while serving
         as the Senior Advisor to the 5th Airborne Battalion, Airborne
         Division, Army of the Republic of Vietnam. When the battalion
         headquarters element Captain McDermott was with came under
         indirect fire and ground attack he twice moved through open
         areas to positions offering unobstructed observation of the
         advancing enemy to direct available tactical air assets on
         the enemy positions and formations. Observed in his second
         position Captain McDermott withstood a heavy volume of fire
         directed at him personally to continued to control the air-
         strikes that destroyed the enemy attack. Captain McDermott's
         display of self-sacrifice, courage and aggressive determination
         was a source of inspiration to his Vietnamese comrades in arms.
         Captain McDermott's conspicuous gallantry in action was in
         keeping with the highest traditions of the United States Army
         and reflects great credit upon himself and the military service.

FOR THE COMMANDER:

OFFICIAL: G. H. WOODWARD
                                                   Major General, USA
                                                   Chief of Staff

JAMES C. GRIFFITH
COL, USA
Chief, Administrative Services

DISTRIBUTION:
  Special

33. Official orders for the Silver Star.

Notes

Preface and Acknowledgments

1. President Nixon attempted to cloak his decision to reverse American policy vis-à-vis Indochina by stressing the importance of concluding the Strategic Arms Limitation Treaty (SALT 1) with the Soviet Union as well as establishing diplomatic relations with the People's Republic of China. He was also deeply concerned about getting reelected. One of the unintended consequences of President Nixon's maneuverings was the North Vietnamese Easter Offensive, a major campaign that included the attack on the provincial capital of An Loc. President Nixon's subsequent resignation took him out of the game and the 93rd Congress, much addicted to self-serving pettifoggery, eventually succeeded in completing the process of gifting Indochina to the enemy.

Chapter 1

1. Opinions on North Vietnamese strategic objectives are mixed and difficult to clarify as they undoubtedly changed as the offensive developed. Philip C. Clarke, "The Battle That Saved Saigon," *Reader's Digest,* March 1973, 151, cites an unidentified North Vietnamese source who named Saigon as the strategic objective while Orrin DeForest and David Chanoff, *Slow Burn: The Rise and Bitter Fall of American Intelligence in Vietnam* (New York: Simon & Schuster, 1990), 197–198, argues that North Vietnamese objectives were limited to seizing territory that would support their negotiations in Paris. Dale Andradé, *America's Last Vietnam Battle: Halting Hanoi's 1972 Easter Offensive* (Lawrence: University Press of Kansas, 2001), 25–26, provides a broader and more-calibrated range of North Vietnamese objectives.

Chapter 2

1. Aeschylus, 525 B.C.–456 B.C., was a celebrated Athenian playwright recognized as the father of Greek tragedy. Many of his plays dealt with warfare, and as a veteran

of the important battles of Marathon and Salamis, where he fought against the Persians, he was an acknowledged expert on the subject.

Chapter 3

1. Stephen P. Randolph, *Powerful and Brutal Weapons: Nixon, Kissinger, and the Easter Offensive* (Cambridge, MA: Harvard University Press, 2007), 15–19, provides an analysis of the major operational problems associated with Lam Son 719 that influenced North Vietnamese planning relevant to the Easter Offensive.

Chapter 6

1. Tran Van Nhut, *An Loc: The Unfinished War* (Lubbock: Texas Tech University Press, 2009), 108–109, describes other events unfolding in the vicinity of Chon Thanh that I was blissfully unaware of.

2. James H. Willbanks, *The Battle of An Loc* (Bloomington: Indiana University Press, 2005), 67.

Chapter 7

1. Andradé, *America's Last Vietnam Battle,* 340–341, provides an excellent introduction to Major General Hollingsworth.

2. Nhut, *An Loc,* 109. The incident is also mentioned by K. G. Mortensen, *The Battle of An Loc: 1972* (Parksville, Australia: Gerald Griffin Press, 1996), 35.

Chapter 12

1. Andradé, *America's Last Vietnam Battle,* 393, states the 1st Airborne Brigade inserted on 13 and 14 April. Willbanks, *The Battle of An Loc,* 87, states the operation occurred on 14 and 15 April, dates that are confirmed by Corley, *Binh Long Province Headquarters Daily Log.*

Chapter 13

1. Corley, *Binh Long Province Headquarters Daily Log,* records that "oilskin" (my call sign) was in contact with the enemy on 16 April.

2. Multiple sources agree that the main attack on the firebase started on 19 April. This account of the 6th Airborne Battalion's fight and subsequent breakout is based on discussions and correspondence with Ross Kelly.

Chapter 15

1. Corley, *Binh Long Province Headquarters Daily Log,* provides an on-the-spot account of the Airborne Ranger attack on 19 April. Their employment is also recorded

by both Nhut, *An Loc,* 129, and Lam Quang Thi, *Hell in An Loc,* (Denton: University of North Texas Press, 2009) 152.

Chapter 16

1. U.S. Air Force colonel (R) Tom Lebar, a B-52 aircraft commander during the Vietnam War and a veteran of numerous missions to An Loc, and Bill Carruthers, a FAC during the battle and a B-52 pilot later, provided the author with many of the specifics concerning the employment and armament of B-52D aircraft included in this vignette. B-52 bombloads were limited only by the capacity of the internal racks and wing hard points. The aircraft were aerially refueled as required, sometimes both on the way to and returning from their targets.

Chapter 17

1. Andradé, *America's Last Vietnam Battle,* 427–435, provides insight into the lead-up to this major North Vietnamese attack from the American perspective, as well as how the response was organized and executed.

2. The two crew members were Captain Rodney Strobridge and Captain Robert Williams. The most recent reporting indicates their remains have not been recovered.

Chapter 18

1. Mortensen, *The Battle of An Loc: 1972,* 47.

2. Pep McPhillips has discussed this event with me several times. Since this is my story I get to recount how Pep's drama looked from where I sat, rather than from where he hung.

Chapter 19

1. The pickup took place after dark on the north edge of the 5th Airborne Battalion's perimeter, about fifty yards from my bunker. An 8th Airborne Battalion advisor was among those evacuated, requiring the American sergeant serving with me to move to that battalion.

Chapter 20

1. Howard R. Simpson, *Dien Bien Phu: The Epic Battle America Forgot* (Washington, D.C.: Brassey's, 1994), 175, describes how harshly Viet Minh captors treated Vietnamese prisoners who had served as paratroopers in the Foreign Legion or the other parachute battalions.

Chapter 21

1. Andradé, *America's Last Vietnam Battle*, 411–419, and Randolph, *Powerful and Brutal Weapons*, 238–240, describe how a system to meet the aerial supply challenge was developed, but the best account is provided by a participant, U.S. Air Force brigadier general (R), then major Ed Byra, in Carruthers, *The Battle of An Loc: A Massive Convergence of Forces*, at www.anloc.org/.

2. Thi, *Hell in An Loc*, 144–154, provides a good overview of the emergency to include the major units involved.

Chapter 25

1. Willbanks, *The Battle of An Loc*, 76, and Andradé, *America's Last Vietnam Battle*, 388, provide detailed descriptions of the North Vietnamese inability to coordinate their combined arms attacks.

2. Andradé, *America's Last Vietnam Battle*, 408.

3. Mortensen, *The Battle of An Loc: 1972*, 47, quoting Braestrup, *The Big Story: How the American Press and Television Reported and Interpreted the Crisis of Tet in Vietnam and Washington* (New Haven, CT: Yale University Press), 263. Bernard B. Fall, *Hell in a Very Small Place* (Cambridge, MA: De Capo Press, 2002), records artillery by type and amount fired by French forces on several specific dates, but no overall numbers. Fall comments on enemy artillery inventories but does not provide any specifics concerning ordnance fired at Dien Bien Phu. Simpson, *Dien Bien Phu: The Epic Battle America Forgot*, 35, lists 144 artillery pieces, 36 antiaircraft guns, and several twelve-tube Katyusha rocket launchers in the communist inventory but does not estimate the volume of ammunition shot at the French forces.

4. Mortensen, *The Battle of An Loc: 1972*, and Bruce B. G. Clarke, *Expendable Warriors: The Battle of Khe Sanh and the Vietnam War* (Mechanicsburg, PA: Stackpole Books, 2007), 102–105, comment on the ground attack that never came and incoming fire that peaked with 1,300 rounds impacting on one day. Clarke stresses the seventy-seven-day length of the Khe Sanh siege, calling it the longest siege of the Vietnam War. Perhaps it was the longest siege for American units, but the main combat base was never subjected to ground attacks supported by tanks, the volumes of incoming fire over the length of time that the troops defending An Loc experienced, or the numbers of both enemy and friendly casualties. Nor did the siege at Khe Sanh last as long; it was three months between the day when enemy tanks crashed into the town of An Loc and the day when Brigadier General Tallman and his party were killed, and the battle was not over with that event.

5. Willbanks, *The Battle of An Loc*, 146.

Chapter 26

1. The best gunship Web sites include Frank Vaughn's http://www.faqs.org/faqs/vietnam/usaf-gunships/ and http://www.theaviationzone.com/factsheets/gunships.asp, hosted by Mike Neely.

2. The Web site Spooky & Puff contains great material at http://www
.ac119gunships.com.

3. The definitive Web site on this aircraft is http://www.spectre-association.org/
historySpectre.htm.

Chapter 28

1. Thi, *Hell in An Loc*, 187.
2. Willbanks, *The Battle of An Loc*, 149.
3. Mortensen, *The Battle of An Loc: 1972*, 28.
4. Willbanks, *The Battle of An Loc*, 146–147.

Chapter 30

1. Thi, *Hell in An Loc*, 237–241, details the subsequent detentions, suicides, execu-
tions, and banishments suffered by many of the South Vietnamese officers who participated in the battle for An Loc. In addition to Thi's recounting, there were many
others who chose to become a Quan Tu, a Virtuous Leader, rather than surrender to
the enemy.

34. A South Vietnamese officer who chose to become a Quan Tu, a Virtuous Leader,
with the fall of Saigon. Photo courtesy of Pham, vnafmamn.

Bibliography

(Military ranks are as of the spring of 1972)

Secondary Sources

AC-119 Gunship Association. *Home of the Vietnam War's Special Operations Squadrons.* http://www.ac119gunships.com/the119s/ac119g.htm.

Andradé, Dale. *America's Last Vietnam Battle: Halting Hanoi's 1972 Easter Offensive.* Lawrence: University Press of Kansas, 2001.

Berman, Larry. *No Peace, No Honor: Nixon, Kissinger, and Betrayal in Vietnam.* New York: Simon & Schuster, 2002.

Carruthers, William. *The Battle of An Loc: A Massive Convergence of Forces,* http://www.anloc.org.

Clarke, Bruce B. G. *Expendable Warriors: The Battle of Khe Sanh and the Vietnam War.* Mechanicsburg, PA: Stackpole Books, 2007.

DeForest, Orrin and David Chanoff. *Slow Burn: The Rise and Bitter Fall of American Intelligence in Vietnam.* New York: Simon & Schuster, 1990.

Fall, Bernard B. *Hell in a Very Small Place.* Cambridge, MA: Da Capo Press, 2002, reprinted by arrangement with Harper and Row, copyright 1966.

Lam Quang Thi. *Hell in An Loc.* Denton: University of North Texas Press, 2009.

Mortensen, K. G. *The Battle of An Loc: 1972.* Parksville, Australia: Gerald Griffin Press, 1996.

Mulligan, Hugh A. *Pacific Stars & Stripes.* Vol. 28, No. 106, p. 1. 16 April 1972.

Neely, Mike. *USAF Fixed Wing Gunships,* http://www.theaviationzone.com/factsheets/.

Nhut, Tran Van, with Christian L. Arevian. *An Loc: The Unfinished War.* Lubbock: Texas Tech University Press, 2009.

Pham, Timothy. Angels in Red Hats. *Portraits of Nhay Du (ARVN AIRBORNE).* http://vnafmamn.com.

Randolph, Stephen P. *Powerful and Brutal Weapons: Nixon, Kissinger, and the Easter Offensive.* Cambridge, MA: Harvard University Press, 2007.

Republic of Vietnam. Ministry of Foreign Affairs. *The Heroic Battle of An Loc.* Saigon, 1972.

Simpson, Howard R. *Dien Bien Phu: The Epic Battle America Forgot*. Washington, D.C.: Brassey's, 1994.

Sorenson, Theodore C. *Let The Word Go Forth: The Speeches, Statements, and Writings of John F. Kennedy—1947 to 1963*. New York: Dell, 1991.

Spectre Association. *Home of the AC-130 Gunships*. http://www.spectreassociation.org/historySpectre.htm.

Spooky & Puff. *Puff the Magic Dragon*. http://www.ac-119gunships.com.

Turley, Gerald H. *The Easter Offensive: The Last American Advisors Vietnam 1972*. Novato, CA: Presidio Press, 1985.

Vaughn, Frank. *soc.history. war. vietnam: USAF Gunships,* http://www.faqs.org/vietnam/usaf-gunships.

VNAF Photos. http://www.vnafmamn.com/vnaf_photos.html.

Willbanks, James H. *The Battle of An Loc*. Bloomington: Indiana University Press, 2005.

Periodicals

Clarke, Philip C. "The Battle That Saved Saigon." *Reader's Digest,* March 1973, pp. 151–156.

Mulligan, Hugh A. "Highway of Death: Thunder Road Paved With Blood." *Pacific Stars & Stripes,* 16 April 1972.

Ulmer, Walter, Colonel. "Notes on Enemy Armor in An Loc." *Armor,* January–February 1973, pp. 15–20.

Monographs/Speeches

Benedit, Edward B., Lieutenant Colonel. U.S. Army. Untitled monograph. http://www.anloc.org.

Byra, Ed, Major. U.S. Air Force. Untitled speech to USAF Airlift Convention about C-130 tactics used at An Loc. http://www.anloc.org.

Corley, Robert, Lieutenant Colonel. U.S. Army. "An Loc Personal Account." http://www.anloc.org.

Howard, John, Major. U.S. Army. "They Were Good Ol' Boys: An Infantryman Remembers An Loc and the Air Force." http://www.anbloc.org.

———. "The War We Came to Fight: A Study of the Battle of An Loc, April–June 1972." Paper written for the Student Research Report, U.S. Army Command & General Staff College, Ft. Leavenworth, KS, June 1974.

Moffett, Harold, Jr., Captain. U.S. Army. "An Loc Personal Account: 7 April 1972 to 31 May 1972." http//www.anloc.org.

Unpublished Primary Sources

Corley, Robert, Lieutenant Colonel. *Binh Long Province Headquarters Daily Log,* 4 April 1972–4 June 1972. Organized by date of entry, unnumbered pages.

Kelly, Ross, First Lieutenant. U.S. Army, Senior Advisor 6th Airborne Battalion, After Action Report of battalion combat operations from the combat assault on

14 April to the eventual pick-up of the battalion's survivors on 21 April, 10 unnumbered pages.

Taylor, Arthur, Lieutenant Colonel. U.S. Army, Senior Advisor 1st Airborne Brigade, After Action Report of brigade combat operations from deployment on 7 April to 21 June when brigade units were returned to their home compounds. Included is a roster of U.S. advisor personnel, casualties by unit, and a list of lessons learned. Pages numbered 1 through 10.

Interviews and Correspondence

Carruthers, William, First Lieutenant. U.S. Air Force, 21st Tactical Air Support Squadron, Forward Air Controller (Sundog 39) at An Loc.

Corley, Robert, Lieutenant Colonel. U.S. Army, Senior Advisor, Binh Long Province Advisory Team headquartered in An Loc.

Hensley, Don, Captain. U.S. Army, Advisor, Binh Long Province Advisory Team.

Howard, John, Major. U.S. Army, Senior Advisor 6th Airborne Battalion. John provided invaluable copies of the two unpublished After Action Reports cited above.

Kelly, Ross, First Lieutenant. U.S. Army, Senior Advisor, 6th Airborne Battalion, ARVN Airborne Division.

Lebar, Tom, Major. U.S. Air Force, B-52 Aircraft Commander, 43rd Bomb Wing, Andersen AFB, Guam. Tom flew multiple An Loc missions.

McPhillips, Pep, First Lieutenant. U.S. Air Force, 21st Tactical Air Support Squadron, Forward Air Controller (Sundog 07) at An Loc.

Todd, Jack, Major. U.S. Army, Senior Advisor 8th Airborne Battalion and Deputy Senior Advisor 1st Airborne Brigade, Vietnamese Airborne Division.

Willbanks, James, Captain. U.S. Army, Advisor TF 52, 18th ARVN Division.

Index

35. This photo of Mike McDermott (left) and a fellow paratrooper was taken during a firefight on 11 November 1967, when Mike was a platoon leader in the 101st Airborne Division. Photo is in the author's collection.